Praise for *My Life as an Experiment*

"Over the years, [Jacobs' experiments] have grown more complex and deeper in potential meaning. Not to mention funnier and funnier."

—*The Kansas City Star*

"[T]he most enlightening moments are driven by his honesty, his sense of humor, and his willingness to constantly challenge his ingrained assumptions. . . . Hilarity, and quite a bit of learning, ensue. . . . In [*My Life as an Experiment*], he once again achieves a rare literary balance—an intellectual study of human behavior that will make readers laugh out loud or, in the more daring cases, inspire them to try one of these experiments for themselves."

—*Providence Journal*

"He's not just in it for the yuks—though there are plenty of yuks. (He's very funny.) He has a curious, questioning mind and is always looking for larger meaning. . . . [*My Life as an Experiment*] is intelligent, insightful shtick."

—*Minneapolis Star-Tribune*

"[*My Life as an Experiment*] is as funny and as instructive as memoir can get."

—*The Knoxville News-Sentinel*

"'Immersive journalism' is a rather popular trope these days, and *Esquire* editor A. J. Jacobs is one of its most entertaining adherents, performing a public service with his quest for knowledge in his latest book, [*My Life as an Experiment*]. . . . His experiments, alternately Herculean and banal, are emblematic of how difficult it is in this modern age to find enlightenment; 'know thyself' regularly brushes up against the cold, rocky bottom of daily life."

—*LA Weekly*

"Jacobs . . . could be the funniest nonfiction writer this side of Bill Bryson. . . . The experiments themselves are fascinating and lead to genuinely surprising conclusions . . . and Jacobs' storytelling is lighthearted and frequently laugh-out-loud funny. . . . There aren't a lot of nonfiction books you want to read over and over, but this is certainly one of them."

—*Booklist* (starred review)

"Jacobs, a kind of latter-day George Plimpton, tests . . . our funny bones once again with his smart-aleck, off-the-wall and uproarious experiments in living."

—*Publishers Weekly*

"Jacobs continues his unique brand of immersion journalism . . . [and] his style is crisp and often laugh-out-loud funny. . . . [An] endearing and nimble look at how pursuing absurd extremes can illuminate the more mundane aspects of contemporary existence."

—*Kirkus Reviews*

ALSO BY A. J. JACOBS

The Know-It-All

The Year of Living Biblically

My Life as an
Experiment

One Man's Humble Quest to Improve Himself by
Living as a Woman, Becoming George Washington,
Telling No Lies, and Other Radical Tests

A. J. Jacobs

Previously published as *The Guinea Pig Diaries*

SIMON & SCHUSTER PAPERBACKS
New York London Toronto Sydney

Simon & Schuster
1230 Avenue of the Americas
New York, NY 10020

First Simon & Schuster trade paperback edition July 2010

SIMON & SCHUSTER PAPERBACKS *and colophon are registered trademarks of*
Simon & Schuster, Inc.

For information about special discounts for bulk purchases,
please contact Simon & Schuster Special Sales at
1-866-506-1949 or business@simonandschuster.com.

The Simon & Schuster Speakers Bureau can bring authors
to your live event. For more information or to book an event
contact the Simon & Schuster Speakers Bureau at
1-866-248-3049 or visit our website at www.simonspeakers.com.

Designed by Davina Mock-Maniscalco

Manufactured in the United States of America

10   9   8   7   6   5   4   3   2   1

The Library of Congress has cataloged the hardcover edition as follows:
Jacobs, A. J., 1968–
My life as an experiment: one man's humble quest to improve himself by living as a
woman, becoming George Washington, telling no lies, and other radical tests / A. J. Jacobs.
   p. cm.
  1. Conduct of life—Humor.   2. Self-actualization (Psychology)—Humor.   I. Title.
PN6231.6142J33   2009
814'.54—dc22   2009024129

ISBN 978-1-4165-9906-7
ISBN 978-1-4391-0499-6 *(pbk)*
ISBN 978-1-4391-1014-0 *(ebook)*

Versions of some of these chapters appeared in Esquire *magazine.*
Previously published as The Guinea Pig Diaries

To Julie

(and also Courtney Holt)

Contents

Introduction

Over the years, I've gotten a lot of suggestions.

Some are intriguing. My brother-in-law suggested I spend a year growing my own food in my Manhattan apartment.

Some are intriguing, but possibly come with a hidden agenda. A friend—at least I think he's a friend—told me I should spend a year without human contact.

Some *definitely* come with an agenda. My wife keeps suggesting that I spend a year giving her foot massages. I usually counteroffer that we could try all the positions in the Kama Sutra. The subject is generally dropped after that.

The suggestions come with the territory. For the last fifteen years, I've attempted to live my life as a human guinea pig. I've engaged in a series of experiments on my mind and body, some of which have been fruitful, some humiliating failures. I've tried to understand the world by immersing myself in extraordinary circumstances. I've also grown a tremendously unattractive beard.

My career as a human guinea pig began with a piece of furniture. I was working at *Entertainment Weekly* magazine in the mid-1990s, and the La-Z-Boy company had just created the most pimped-out, excessive chair in the history of human seating. It pushed the concept of leisure—or sloth, if you are feeling moral—to unheard-of extremes. It had a butt massager, a heater, a built-in fridge for you to store beers and cheese sticks, a modem jack—everything but a toilet and an outboard motor.

I figured the only way to address this magnificent monstrosity was to road test it. See how it held up under severe conditions. Being a committed journalist, I offered to spend twenty-four hours watching TV in this La-Z-Boy and then write about it.

The experiment was actually a bit of a bust. Somewhere in the middle of a *Law & Order* marathon at 3 A.M., I fell asleep for five hours. But I glimpsed the possibilities this type of journalism offered. I was hooked. Since then, I've put myself (and my patient wife) through a battery of experiments, the highlights and lowlights of which are in this book.

To understand the global phenomenon that is outsourcing, I outsourced everything in my life. I hired a team of people in Bangalore, India, to answer my phone, answer my e-mail, argue with my spouse for me. This, by the way, was probably the best month of my life.

To explore the meaning of Truth, I decided to practice something called Radical Honesty. I spent a month without lying. But more than that, I vowed to say whatever popped into my head. No filter between the brain and the mouth. This, by the way, was probably the worst month of my life.

To slow the descent of my rapidly plummeting IQ, I read the *Encyclopædia Britannica* from A to Z. To try to understand religion, I lived by the rules of the Bible, from the Ten Commandments all the way down to stoning adulterers.

I've been told—many, many times—that there are easier ways to make a living.

Which is true.

But I'm addicted to these experiments. I've come to believe that if you really want to learn about a topic, you should get on-the-job training. You should dive in and try to live that topic. If you're interested in Rome, you can look at maps and post-cards and read census data. Or you can actually go to Italy and taste the pesto gnocchi. As the old saying goes: To understand the Italians, you must walk a mile in their loafers.

You have to be interested in the topic. That's rule number one. If you aren't passionate, it shows. But if you are committed to the possibility of change, then there's nothing like it. And these experiences have, in fact, transformed my life for good. I may not keep everything from each experiment—after my year of living biblically, I decided to shave my beard and hang up my robe and sandals. But I do still observe the Sabbath, I still say prayers of thanksgiving every day (even though I'm an agnostic, go figure), and I still try not to covet and gossip, with varying degrees of success.

The goal is that you're able to keep the good parts and not descend into insanity. That the pain of the experiment will end up making life better in the end. And that your spouse will forgive you. For, as I've been told many times, my wife is a saint. A saint, I might add, who doesn't tolerate these experiments lying down. (With the encyclopedia project, for instance, she fined me a dollar for every irrelevant fact that I inserted into conversation.)

Partly, of course, I'm drawn to these experiments because I'm a writer. And a writer who is cursed with a relatively un-eventful upbringing. My dad was not a carny or a drunk or a spy, as far as I know. My ordinary life doesn't merit a book. So I put myself into extraordinary situations, and see what happens.

I've always loved the genre. One of my literary idols is George Plimpton. He's the Dante of participatory journalism. For the sake of the story, he's been sacked by a Detroit Lions defensive lineman and punched in the face by boxer Archie Moore. Before him was method writer John Howard Griffin, who chemically darkened his skin to see how it felt to be a black man in the 1950s South. And even before that came an amazing nineteenth-century journalist named Nellie Bly. Her experiments ranged from the madcap—when Jules Verne's book *Around the World in Eighty Days* came out, she decided to try to replicate the stunt—to the serious—she had herself committed to an infamous New York insane asylum to expose the abuses there.

And when I read the encyclopedia, I found a whole other breed of heroes who experimented on themselves for actual science—usually because no one else would volunteer. There's a great nineteenth-century doctor named Jesse William Lazear, who allowed himself to be bitten by a yellow fever–infected mosquito to show that the insects were spreading the disease. He died proving himself right. And there's Sasha Shulgin, the Thomas Edison of psychedelics. A true mad scientist based in Berkeley, California (of course), the eighty-four-year-old chemist has invented 230 different hallucinogenic drugs. He has ingested each of them himself. "It is like opening a door to a hallway that has unopened doors for its entire length, and beyond every door is a world with which you are totally unfamiliar."

I haven't taken drugs since college. But I know exactly what he means about opening doors. That's what I've tried to do in my career and in this book, *My Life as an Experiment*. I hope you like what I've found behind them.

$$\text{Fame} \leq \text{Ego}\,(x)^3$$

$$\frac{\text{Zen} + \text{Focus} = \text{Productivity}^2}{\sqrt{\text{Brain}} \cdot \text{Caveman}} = \frac{1}{x}$$

$$\frac{\text{Outsourcing}^8 + \text{marriage}}{12{,}000 \text{ miles}} = 9$$

$$x = \frac{\text{Nudity} + \text{Public}}{\text{Dignity}}$$

$$\sqrt{\frac{\text{Nudity} + \text{Public}}{\text{Dignity}}}$$

$$(\text{Geo. Wash.} - \text{Wig})\,\text{Me} = x$$

$$\frac{\text{Dating} + \text{Beauty}}{x\,(\text{Cyrano})} \neq \text{Love}$$

$$\int_b^a \frac{\text{husband}}{(\text{wife})\,\text{power}}$$

$$(\text{wife})\,\text{power}^3 = x$$

$$\frac{\text{Reason} - \text{Emotion}}{\text{Behavior}} = \text{Insanity}$$

$$\text{Truth}^n - \text{filter} = \text{Chaos}$$

Chapter One

The Unitasker

I'm writing this chapter with the stereo silent. The TV black. The room dark. The pinging of the e-mails silenced. I am focused on nothing else but this glowing computer screen, the blinking cursor, and the words appearing in Helvetica twelve-point font.

I'm not paying attention to the honking taxis on the street, or the clanking drum solo of my radiator. I'm certainly not paying attention to my two-year-old son, Zane, who is outside my office door, apparently doing an impression of Fran Drescher impersonating Alvin the Chipmunk.

I'm trying to do this because I realize I have a problem focusing. My brain is all over the place.

Consider this: multitasking almost killed me. Maybe I'm being melodramatic here. You be the judge. Two years ago, Julie and I were driving a rented Taurus to my cousin's wedding in Woodstock, New York. The kids were at home with our babysitter, Michelle.

I was at the wheel, weaving my way north, listening to the audio book we'd brought along: the biography of Albert Einstein by Walter Isaacson. It's a good book. Dangerously good.

Interesting, I thought to myself, as we listened to chapter 8.

When Einstein was a clerk at the patent office, he did a lot of work on clocks that were synchronized at the speed of light, which led to his early ideas on relativity. His day job was crucial. If he'd been a regular old tenured professor, we might not have relativity and our kids would be watching videos called *Baby Heisenberg*.

I'm not a fan of driving. I know a lot of people get a dopamine rush from steering a powerful steel machine down a road. I've seen the postcoitally blissful faces of men in Honda commercials. But for me, driving holds all the allure of operating an electric can opener. In other words, I found the life of the world's greatest scientist more intriguing than the Saw Mill River Parkway.

My mind drifted from the road. The car drifted from the road. Julie screamed.

I snapped my attention back to the highway and jammed the steering wheel hard to the left. Tires squealed. An overcorrection. Now to the right. We serpentined for a few seconds, then hit the shoulder and launched into space. We jumped a waist-high concrete median and bounced down ass-backward into oncoming traffic on the other side of the highway. A "real *Dukes of Hazzard*" move, as the tow truck driver later described it. If only Julie had been wearing jean shorts.

We sat for a few seconds in our rental car, the bottom ripped off, the hood crinkled. For reasons only weird Einsteinian physics can explain, no other cars smashed into us. I was relieved to still be breathing. Julie was crying—somewhat relieved, but mostly furious at me for losing control. The rest of the afternoon consisted of cops, rental car insurance forms, rubberneckers, and strained silence. We were three hours late for the wedding.

Julie has since banned me from all driving except in parking lots and cul-de-sacs. On road trips out of New York, I get to sit in the back and negotiate peace treaties about which Nickelodeon movie we're going to put in the portable DVD player. That may seem like it's emasculating, but is just fine with me. I know I'm a terrible driver.

My near-death experience put an end, at least for now, to my driving career. But it didn't put a speed bump in my multitasking habits. Not a bit. Unless I'm doing at least two things at once, I feel like I'm wasting my time. Phone and e-mail. Watching *The Office,* checking Facebook, and reading the *Times* op-eds online. Texting and peeing.

My friend Andy taught me how to read-walk. He could read an entire *Newsweek* magazine on his walk from the subway to his apartment. Just be sure to glance up once every paragraph or two, he told me.

I recently read a quote from actress Jennifer Connelly in *The Atlantic:* "I do like to read a book while having sex. And talk on the phone. You can get so much done." Julie would never go for that. But I do remember a girlfriend who allowed *Law & Order* to play in the background, which made for some efficient, suspense-filled romance, with a plot twist at 10:41 P.M.

In one sense, task-juggling makes me feel great: busy, energized, fulfilled, like I'm living three lives in the space of one.

But I also know I'm scattered. I'm overloading my circuits. I know, deep down, this overstimulated, underfocused world is driving us all batty. My mom—who complains when I click through my e-mails while talking to her on the phone (and by talking, I mean that I toss out an occasional "uh-huh," and "sounds good")—recently sent me a *Times* article about how multitasking is actually inefficient.

Hence Operation Focus. I'm going to recapture my attention

span, which currently can be measured only by one of those atomic clocks. I pledge to go cold turkey from multitasking for a month. Only single tasks. Unitasking. And just as important, I'll stick with each task for more than my average thirty seconds. I'll be the most focused man in the world.

THE PREPARATION

I collected a shelfful of books on attention. I won't even mention how hard it was to focus on them. (Note to William James: I love you, but easy on the dependent clauses, please!)

What I took away was this: when I said multitasking is a life-or-death problem, I wasn't exaggerating. And not just because Driving Under the Influence of Text Messaging causes 630,000 crashes a year. The stakes are even higher. We're talking survival of civilization itself—at least if you believe some of these writers. Author Maggie Jackson wrote an intriguing and frightening book called *Distracted: The Erosion of Attention and the Coming Dark Age.*

Okay, maybe "Dark Age" is a tad alarmist. I don't think we're going to stop reading books and start waging religious wars. Umm, let me rephrase. Let's just say I think "Dark Age" might be an overstatement. But the gist of Jackson's book is right. The culture of distraction is changing the way we think. It's rewiring our brains. It's making it harder for us to solve complex problems. Nicholas Carr writes in *The Atlantic* in an article called "Is Google Making Us Stupid?" (hint: yes), "Once I was a scuba diver in the sea of words. Now I zip along the surface like a guy on a Jet-Ski."

Our hopscotching brains make us more depressed (it's harder to focus on the positive), less able to connect with people and form a conscience. And our attention spans are to blame for

America's dismal math skills. Malcolm Gladwell points out in *Outliers* that Japanese kids stick with a hard math problem for fourteen minutes, while American kids give up after 9.5 minutes.

Oh, and it's all an insane delusion, to boot. Multitasking makes us feel efficient. But my mom is right: it actually just slows our thinking down. In fact, *multitasking* is the wrong word. Our brains can't handle more than one higher cognitive function at a time. We may think we're multitasking, but we're actually switchtasking. Toggling between one task and another. First the phone, then the e-mail, then the phone, back to the e-mail. And each time you switch, there's a few milliseconds of startup cost. The neurons need time to rev up.

Multitasking costs the economy $650 billion a year, according to the Institute of Pulling Numbers Out of Its Ass. (That's a real estimate, though not the institute's real name.) Whatever the actual total is, I'm starting to think this isn't a problem along the lines of love handles or bad cell service. This is the Eleventh Plague.

THE START

Today is my first day without multitasking. When I get up, I take a shower. That's it. No NPR on the shower radio. It's weirdly quiet, just the sound of water splashing into the tub.

Embrace the stillness, I say to myself. Feel the water on my face. Experience it. Be present. Be mindful.

My brain is not cooperating. *What the hell is going on?* it whines. It sounds a lot like my kids in the backseat demanding a Berenstain Bears DVD. *Where's my damn stimulation?*

I sit at my desk and read the newspaper. That's all. Without checking my e-mails or eating breakfast at the same time. Simply flipping the pages.

This is awful. I feel like my brain has entered a school zone and has to slow down to 25 mph.

My plan is to leave my BlackBerry off till noon. I break down at eleven-thirty.

At lunchtime, Julie and I are in the kitchen.

"Somehow the liquid soap in the bathroom dispenser disappeared," she says.

I stop what I'm doing—making a peanut butter and raspberry jam sandwich—and look at her. Must unitask.

"So I filled it up with soap from the kitchen. And I was washing my hands with it, and it smelled weird."

I'm watching her face. Maybe staring too much. That reminds me. I have to call the Fox publicist about their new show on reading people's faces. Focus, Jacobs!

"It smelled . . . industrial. And I realized I had used dishwasher liquid instead of regular soap."

It's not that the topic isn't interesting. As someone obsessed with handwashing, this is actually relevant stuff. It's just that I'm usually doing something else during a conversation. Picking up stray cups, or putting away sweaters.

"So I bring it back to the kitchen because I don't want to waste it, and I'm cleaning the coffee pot . . ."

Keep looking at the face. You know, I've always fantasized about inventing contact lenses with tiny TVs embedded in them. You could be looking straight at your coworker as he tells you about his trip to Knott's Berry Farm, but little does he know, on the inside of your contact lens, you're enjoying CSI: Miami. *Just remember to nod occasionally.*

". . . and the suds won't go away. I had to wash the coffee pot for five minutes."

Or braille. I'd always wanted to learn braille. That way I could be having lunch with my boss, making polite noises, while my fingertips read the latest Andrew Jackson biography underneath the table.

"And the coffee still tasted soapy," says Julie.

"Why are you writing that down?" she asks.

"It's for a project."

"Is everything I say fodder?"

I shrugged.

She makes a pouty face. "I'm not just a character."

THE DECLINE AND FALL OF WESTERN ATTENTION

Baboons have a better attention span than I do. This is true. My favorite theory about attention comes from a baboon study. Male baboons, it argues, evolved attention partly so that they could guard the female baboon for a good long time after sex, to make sure no one else conducted any monkey business that might interfere with their sperm. (My question: If this is true, why are men so opposed to cuddling?)

However it started, attention had a decent run in humans for a couple of millennia there. In the book *Distracted*, I read about "attention athletes" such as eighteenth-century Swiss entomologist Charles Bonnet, who "studied a single aphid from 5:30 a.m. to 11 p.m. for twenty-one days straight in order to learn about its reproductive cycle." That guy is my new hero.

Oh to be born in the golden age of attention. When Lincoln and Douglas could have three-hour debates, or the faithful could pray without ceasing for four hours. When people would look at a painting for an afternoon. Paintings! They're like TV, but they don't move.

Then it all broke down. The Industrial Revolution came. We began to fetishize speed and equate quickness with intelligence. We bought into the myth that, as writer Walter Kirn puts it, nonstop connectedness equals freedom. We started to chop everything down into component parts. And worship at the altar of Frederick Taylor and other efficiency experts with clipboards and stopwatches.

I used to be proud of my attention deficit. Or at least I pretended to be proud. Focusing on only one thing for a long time? That went out of style with snuff boxes. I'm part of a new generation, *man*.

I loved to Jet-Ski across the surface. Even when I read the encyclopedia—my longest attempt at sustained focus—it actually fed right into my ADD personality. Each essay is a bite-size nugget. Bored with Abilene, Texas? Here comes abolitionism. Tired of that? Not to worry, the Abominable Snowman's lurking right around the corner.

I still think it's got its advantages. It helped me when I chose articles for *Esquire*. As an editor, if a story grabbed me, I knew it had to be interesting, since my brain was tugged in forty-two directions.

The first hint I was missing something came during my biblical year. The Sabbath—which I still try to practice—taught me the value of stillness.

The science drove it home. In another excellent antimultitasking article in *The Atlantic* (that magazine is all over this beat!), Kirn explains the problem with frightening clarity. Multitasking shortchanges the higher regions of the brain, the ones devoted to learning and memory.

Kirn describes a recent UCLA study:

[R]esearchers asked a group of 20-somethings to sort index cards in two trials, once in silence and once while simultaneously listening for specific tones in a series of randomly presented sounds.

The subjects sorted the cards just as successfully in both trials. But here's the key: when they had the distracting tones in the background, they had a much more difficult time remembering what they were sorting.

It comes down to the brain's real estate: "The subjects' brains coped with the additional task by shifting responsibility from the hippocampus—which stores and recalls information—to the striatum, which takes care of rote, repetitive activities."

And speaking of the brain, Kirn writes: "Even worse, certain studies find that multitasking boosts the level of stress-related hormones such as cortisol and adrenaline and wears down our systems through biochemical friction, prematurely aging us. In the short term, the confusion, fatigue, and chaos merely hamper our ability to focus and analyze, but in the long term, they may cause it to atrophy."

In short, multitasking rots your skull.

Of course, not all multitasking is created equal. It helps if one of the tasks requires less intellectual wattage. If you're mopping the floor while talking on the phone, it's a lot better than texting while on the phone. But even with the mopping, you're eating away at attention. Your conversation will suffer, if only mildly.

THE ODYSSEUS STRATEGY

I've got to do something about my desk. This is where most of my crimes against focus occur.

There's a great *Onion* headline: EMPLOYEE'S MULTITASKING

DOESN'T INCLUDE WORK. That's the way I'm feeling these days. My book is way overdue. My editor keeps sending me e-mails that say, "How's writing?" the subtext being, "Turn in your book this week or you'll be publishing it on your Epson printer and binding it at the copy center."

It's just that there are so many temptations. So many needs to fulfill. Snacks, cups of water, caffeine, curiosity about what Julie's doing. I pop up from my desk once every five minutes.

I'm in Day Four of the experiment, and I decide to engage in some light bondage. It worked for Odysseus. During Project Rationality, I read about how Odysseus demanded his sailors tie him to the mast so that he wouldn't take a swan dive off the starboard side when he heard the alluring singing of the Sirens.

Eminently rational. So in an homage to Odysseus, I've tied myself to the gray Aeron chair in front of my computer. I tried to use my leather belt, but it didn't fit. Instead I'm running a long black extension cord behind the chair and knotting it five times in my lap. It feels kind of safe, like a seat belt.

Five minutes ago, I thought of adjusting the lamp, since the bulb was spotlighting my face like I was about to sing a solo in *A Chorus Line*. But then I'd have to unknot the cord and get up. I keep my butt in the chair and return to my computer. It's working!

"A.J.!" Julie wants something.

"What's up!" I start untying myself.

"A.J.?"

She opens the door to my office and catches me fiddling with the cord. She furrows her brow. She looks at my computer to see if I'm signed on to a site that requires you to be at least eighteen years of age.

"For a project?"

"Uh-huh."

I'm trying not to tell her about my plans in advance, not even the topics of my experiments, so her reactions can be more rigorously scientific. She's stopped asking questions.

"When you're, um, finished, can you get down the small suitcase?"

If you can tolerate the skeptical looks, I strongly recommend the tying yourself down. I finished off large chunks of my book in the last two hours.

It helps that I'm blocking out an equally tempting siren: the Internet.

I will not be checking the Hasbro website to see how many marbles we've lost from Hungry Hungry Hippos. Which could lead to an animated YouTube movie of the green Hungry Hippo singing "Bohemian Rhapsody." Which might lead to the Wayne and Garth "Bohemian Rhapsody" scene. Which then could lead to a page about the scandal caused when Wayne made unkind remarks about Chelsea Clinton. Well, I won't do it again.

Because I've made accessing the Internet an enormous hassle. Simply turning it off isn't enough for me. I'd just go back and turn it on. Instead I went into my system preferences and went trigger happy. I clicked a bunch of random tabs and buttons until I was disconnected from my wireless. I did actually get some work done. My brain was still craving stimulation—I keep clicking on the Firefox icon wistfully. But I know the dry spell is good for me.

Oh, and those four minutes it took me to get back on the Internet at the end of the day—that was collateral damage.

(Note: My hard drive crashed during one of these games of Russian roulette. I'm not sure whether it was the fault of the Russian roulette. But if it was, then it cost me another six hours on the phone with Apple tech support, during which time they said such unwelcome phrases as "That's not good" and "I've never heard of that happening before." So the jury's still out on this method.)

JUST SIT

Studies show that perhaps the best way to improve your focus and learn to unitask is by meditating. There's something called an executive system—it's the part of the brain that oversees where your attention goes, like the conductor of a symphony. Meditation is like going to conducting school.

So a week into my quest, I take the subway to Greenwich Village and ride an elevator up to the Zendo on the eleventh floor. It's as I expected it—a lot of white walls, blond wood, a statue of Buddha.

Today is beginner's class, and there are eight students—all of us men. Which is odd. I never considered meditation up there in the list of manly pursuits next to fantasy league hockey and invading countries. But here we are, eight males, ready to kick some meditation butt.

The teacher is named Derek, and looks exactly like Jimmy Carter, if Jimmy Carter were to put on a pair of loose black pants and a T-shirt with Japanese characters.

"Let's bow to our pillows," says Derek.

Each of us dutifully presses his palms together and bows to his assigned round, chocolate-colored cushion. We sit down in a circle.

My fellow meditators are all in their twenties, thirties, and forties. A couple have come straight from the office, their ties loosened but intact. They look like they've taken a hammering from the S&P 500 and are hoping to find some ancient Eastern-style peace.

"Tonight, we're going to sit. That's what meditation is all about—sitting." Derek's voice is Mister Rogers–style soothing. I guess that's a job requirement. You can't teach deep relaxation if you sound like Gilbert Gottfried, which means I can scratch it off my list of potential careers.

Derek talks calmly and wisely. He talks about how meditation helps us slow down and see the "amazingness of the universe" and the beauty of koans. "You have to appreciate your life," he says. "The pain, the struggles, the farts."

We men chuckle. After fifteen minutes he asks, "Does anyone have any questions? Because I could ramble on all day."

I raise my hand. I like musings and fart references as much as the next guy, but I want to get to the meat. So I say, "Can you tell us the technique for meditating? Some tips?"

"I'm going to get to that," he said. There was just a tiny ripple of annoyance in his pond of serenity.

"Oh. Sorry."

I'm chastened. Not so Zen of me.

Derek does give us some simple marching orders—sit up straight, keep your eyes open but don't focus on anything, try not to move. Our starter gun is a wooden chime that he knocks. And we're off on a fifteen-minute sit.

I sit. And sit, staring at the floor in the middle of the circle. I listen to the guy next to me breathe. He's breathing loudly. Really loudly. Like Darth Vader. With asthma. During heavy foreplay.

It makes me self-conscious about my own inhaling and exhaling. I'm a heavy breather myself. When we were growing up and watching TV together, my sister would tell me to stop breathing so loudly. I'd make an elaborate show of holding my breath, then after half a minute I'd say, "Would it be okay to inhale now, ma'am?"

It's just a sound, this wheezing. Rise above it. Don't focus on it.

Tock-tock. Derek hits the wooden chime again.

"How'd everyone do?" he asks.

"Great." "Really good." "Good."

I say nothing, too ashamed to confess.

A few minutes later, we try our second and final sit. This time we've graduated from the bunny slope. It'll be twenty minutes, we'll be facing the wall, and we'll be counting our breaths.

Things go a bit better. I'm not annoyed by the background noises, the taxis, and the sighs. I let them flow in one ear and out the other. But I still can't settle my mind. My monkey mind, as they call it in meditation.

The thoughts keep pinging around in my skull. Dozens of them. I think of my aunt's bizarre ex-husband Gil, who spent months meditating on an ashram, and who claims in his autobiography that the Maharishi Mahesh Yogi "couldn't keep his hands off Mia Farrow's butt." *Eighty-two. Eighty-three.* I think of the time I went to see Buddhist poet Gary Snyder speak in Berkeley, and how he said he liked to go to museums and stare at the white spaces in between the paintings. *One hundred four. One hundred five.*

I wonder what's the highest anyone has ever counted in meditation. What if you get up to the millions? Would you still be able to say the numbers in one breath?

I haven't quite got the hang of this yet. I leave the Zendo at the same time as one of the guys with a tie, who proceeds to fart in the elevator.

DINNER WITHOUT DISTRACTION

"Can we eat dinner tonight without multitasking?" I ask, a couple of days later.

"What does that mean?" Julie says.

"No TV. Just a quiet dinner."

"Sounds nice."

"Also, no talking to each other. I just want to concentrate on eating."

Julie is sitting on the bed. She collapses her head on her knees.

"Why do you choose the worst times to ask me these things?" She's had a long day, and is in no mood to sit in silence.

"It's for the project."

"Fine."

I put out the plates and we each take some spoonfuls of the vegetable pad thai we ordered.

"I'm at least going to call my mom," she says.

"No. You can't. That'd distract our focus."

We sit across from each other. I smile and chew.

It reminds me of this astounding passage from George Washington's letters. At one point, he wrote, he and Martha had not had dinner at home alone for twenty years. Every night for twenty years—7,300 days in a row—they had guests and visiting dignitaries to entertain.

Julie's and my guests were TV characters. How long has it been since we've eaten together at home without firing up the TiVo to *30 Rock* or a *Mad Men*?

We're silent for several minutes. Julie nods at me. I nod back.

"This feels very *Revolutionary Road*," Julie says.

I laugh. I know she thinks the whole experiment is absurd.

"No talking, please," I say.

I concentrate on my pad thai. The salt, the crunch, the grease.

"This isn't so bad," I say. "It's relaxing."

"No talking," she says.

Julie once told me that every month or so, she'll look at me and think, "Hey, that's A. J. Jacobs from the twenty-eighth floor. What the hell is he doing here in my house?"

We met when we both worked at *Entertainment Weekly*—I was on the twenty-eighth floor, she was on the twenty-ninth. We knew each other as colleagues for five years before our first date.

I'm looking at Julie across the table, and I'm having a "Hey, that's Julie Schoenberg from the twenty-ninth floor" moment.

"I'm glad I met you," I say.

"No talking."

EXTREME FOCUS

The next morning, I decide to track down a unitasker par excellence. During my biblical year, I'd run across a job called a sofer. These are the Jewish scribes who copy the Bible one painstaking letter at a time. A single Bible can take years to finish. And the stakes are high. If your attention wanders and you make an errant stroke while writing the name of G-d, you have to start the whole section again, losing hours or maybe days.

This, I figure, is Extreme Focus.

I find a sofer on the Internet and dial him up. I put the phone to my ear and shut my eyes. That's how I'm talking on the phone nowadays. I'm a Blind Caller. Remember those Mesozoic days when people actually sat and talked on the phone—just talked? I'm trying to re-create that. The key is to close the eyes and remove temptation. So much less stressful. It's a blissful freedom from choice that leads to phone conversations with actual substance.

He answers. I explain my project.

"I'm Xeroxing something," he says. "Can I call you back in five minutes?"

An hour later, my cell phone chimes.

"Okay, that was more than five minutes. I don't know if you work in an office where you have to go somewhere to . . ." He pauses. "Come in!" Another pause. "Oh, I need to sign this. Okay, the signature here?

"I'm going to put the phone down for one minute," Neil says.

In the background, I hear shuffling.

"Have you seen my calendar downstairs?" Neil shouts to someone.

Hmm. Is this the right man to talk to about sustained focus?

Twenty minutes and several interruptions later, we've arranged to meet next Monday at the Applejack Diner in midtown.

Neil looks a bit like a yarmulke-clad Harvey Fierstein. He's wearing a striped blue shirt and a gray vest. A former advertising man, he became a scribe twenty-five years ago. And his handwriting is beautiful. When he writes down my address to send me a book, it appears on the page full of swirls and flourishes. My ZIP code looks as elegant as the Preamble to the Constitution.

It takes him up to a year to write a Torah, working ten hours a day. Has his head hit the board from exhaustion? Yes. But he does love it. "When the scribe is not present, the letter is not alive. It just becomes a series of strokes."

When I ask him how he keeps from being bored, he shows

me by taking out a calligraphy pen and a piece of paper. Each letter can be viewed from a thousand different angles. The shape of the letters—the slender, graceful Italian style or the blockier Czech look. You can think of the frequency the letters appear in. Or how the letter relates to its original pictogram. He speaks quickly, excitedly.

That's the secret to getting into the state of flow—being totally in love with your topic. I remember I once met an ornithologist who was visiting my grandfather's house. The man stood at the back door with a stoned-like smile on his face for an hour, just watching the birds.

I'm not in a state of flow. I'm battling a nasty cold, and can barely keep my eyelids from drooping as Neil talks about the personality of the different letters. I tune out, coming in occasionally to hear things like "The orange juice *is* there, *was* there, and always *will* be there."

To keep myself engaged, I ask him another question: How do you keep from making errors?

"You can't think about it. You're going to mess up. So what? You start over. If you want to avoid making a mistake, you cannot try to avoid making a mistake. You just have to forget about it."

I know what he means. It's a strange tic of our brain. Sometimes, the more goal-oriented we are, the *less likely* we are to attain that goal. If you really, really want something, you have to forget how much you want it. Or else you'll be too nervous to get it. But dear Lord, that's a cruel and paradoxical system evolution has devised.

And it invades even the lowliest of human endeavors. If I'm standing next to my boss at the urinal and really want to pee, I can't think about peeing. If I say, "Okay, now pee," I'll be standing there till the building closes down. I have to think about, say, the color of the wall. Sometimes, it seems, you can pay too much attention.

A week ago, Julie and I went to see *Doubt*. And Philip Seymour Hoffman's charismatic priest (who may or may not have done something horrible) teaches the basketball team how to toss a free throw. He says you can't think about throwing the free throw, or you'll get too nervous. You have to have a routine. Bend your knees. Bounce the ball twice. Whatever it is, do it every time. And you'll be thinking of your routine and you'll forget to be nervous.

Sometimes, you have to focus on the trees, not the forest.

BOUNDARIES

My cell phone rings. It's my mom.

"A.J., I'm trying to buy Julie a present for—"

"Can I call you back?"

She seems a little put out. I usually talk to her, seeing as I'm not an air traffic controller and can take a couple of minutes out of my day.

"It's just that these are work hours," I explain.

It's two-thirty in the afternoon and I'm trying to be one of the only people in America who still works a nine-to-five job. I want to work, then stop. I don't punch a clock, but I do jot down my starting and ending time.

"I'll call you at five-fifteen."

Maggie Jackson, the author of *Distracted*, says it's essential to set borders around work. She does it physically, by sitting down, stretching her arms, and saying to herself, Okay, this is work time.

I call back at five-fifteen. Then Julie and I have dinner. Then I go back to work at eight-thirty. Workaholism is a hard disease to cure.

THE WISDOM OF GURU BILL MURRAY

I am in line at the corner deli to buy a Diet Coke. So naturally, I say to myself, "I'm waiting in line to buy a Diet Coke." I speak it out loud, as confidently as I can.

The guy in front of me—wearing a CBS Sports hat—swivels his head.

"I'm looking around the store," I continue. "I see a stack of oranges and bananas."

He looks at my head for an earpiece. Maybe a Bluetooth headset to reassure himself that I'm on the phone. Nope. I'm just talking to myself.

"And now I'm getting my wallet out of my pants."

He looks at me like, well, like he's just seen a child vomit into an Easter basket.

It's all part of my new strategy for unitasking. It's a strange one, but it does have scientific backing. I call it the Bill Murray Method of Extreme Focus.

Maybe you remember the scene in *Caddyshack*? The one in which Murray's whackjob, gopher-hunting greenskeeper pretends to be playing golf. He's got a gardening tool and he's thwacking these fancy white flowers outside the clubhouse, sending the petals spraying. All the while, he's also pretending to be a sportscaster covering the event. He's providing his own real-time color commentary:

"Incredible Cinderella story. This unknown, comes out of nowhere, to lead the pack at Augusta . . . [thwacks a flower] . . .

The normally reserved Augusta crowd, going wild . . . he's gonna hit about a five iron it looks like. He's got a beautiful backswing [thwack] . . . oh, he got all of that one! He's got to be pleased with that . . . [thwack] It looks like a mirac—IT'S IN THE HOLE! IT'S IN THE HOLE! Former greenskeeper, now Masters champion.

After I saw *Caddyshack* when I was twelve, I started to do the same thing whenever I played sports by myself (which was my preferred way to play sports, since it cut down on the chances of losing). "Jacobs bounces the ball. He shoots! He scores! Un-bah-liev-able!"

I liked the idea of a crowd cheering me on. It jacked up the excitement. So I started to expand the self-narration to other activities. Why should sports have all the fun? "Jacobs has the Tater Tot in sight," I'd say when eating at the brown Formica table at the cafeteria. "He spears it with his fork. Jim, will you look at that? Exquisite form. He is a master. Down goes that Tater Tot! Down goes the Tater Tot!"

I weaned myself from sportscasting my own life in high school. But now, during Project Focus, I've brought it back with force. Well, at least a version of it. I've cut down on the "crowd goes wild" and I've switched from "Jacobs" to first person. But I'm narrating my own existence.

If I go to the bathroom, I say, "I'm going to the bathroom." I know I sound like Rain Man. But I'm telling you, it's changed my life.

First, it's a good torch to keep away the multitasking monsters. If I start to absentmindedly multitask, I'll be the first to know. No secrets from myself.

But more than that, it's Buddhist enlightenment by way of Bob Costas. More specifically:

- It forces you to live a mindful life. You are present. "I am walking through Central Park. I'm in the middle of a crowded city, and I can barely see the buildings, barely hear the traffic, just trees and jutting rocks and grass. Amazing." It makes me thankful for nature and New York and Frederick Law Olmsted. When I interview attention researcher Meredith Minear from the College of Idaho, she says I stumbled onto an ancient technique. Part of the reason that evolution developed vocalizing was to hone our attention.

- It helps balance your emotions. The very act of saying "I'm angry" makes you less angry. It lights up the language centers in the brain, which are in the more evolved cerebral cortex, which allows you to better control yourself. When you label something, you gain a level of mastery over it. You'll still be pissed, you may still want to smack that person with numchucks, but you'll have a little distance and perspective.

- It tips you off to warped thinking. The other day, Julie told me she left her *New York* magazine in one of the suitcases she took on a weekend trip, but she couldn't remember which. I searched the first, then the second, then the third. I found the magazine in the third suitcase. "Of course, it's in the third," I said out loud. "That's my luck." I paused. "Actually, maybe that's not my luck. I learned from my Rationality Project, my luck is average. It's just that I remember the unlucky incidents more often."

"I'm bringing you the *New York* magazine," I said.

"I see that," Julie said.

"I'm handing it to you, my wife, and then I'm going to leave the room."

"Thanks for the update!"

"I'm noticing the painting in our living room for the first time in two years. It's nice and bright and yellow."

"Good to know."

She'd already started to read the magazine.

VIRTUAL SITTING

Yesterday, I made a crucial discovery: Wii Fit offers a meditation video game. A video game! And here I had been trying to do it in real life without electronic equipment, like some loser from the eighth century.

The "game" is called "Lotus Focus," and the idea is to watch a pixellated candle flicker onscreen while you are sitting on a Wii sensor board. And then continue sitting really still. If you move, you lose.

I crossed my legs, sat down, and pressed start. Forty-three seconds later, I must have shifted a butt muscle. The game finished with a curt sayonara.

Until they add a secret trapdoor where you can enter an opium den and flirt with geisha girls, Lotus Focus is probably not going to outsell *Grand Theft Auto IV*. It's basically a really expensive version of Statues—a "game" my mom made us play at my seventh birthday when we kids got too rowdy. Same goal: stay really still. At least Statues had candy prizes involved at the end. (Incidentally, I found out the ultimate cheat on Lotus Focus. I packed up a suitcase with books and put it on the Wii sensor board. Can't get much stiller. A winner every time! What is the sound of one hand high-fiving, suckah?)

So Wii is not the path to enlightenment. I'm going to have to keep meditating without electronic devices. Which is why, for half an hour each night, I've been sitting on some scrunched-up pillows, lowering my lids to half-mast, cupping my hands in my lap, and trying to do it old school.

The first four or five times I thought I might die of boredom. I fell asleep twice, once with my eyes open. I also tipped backward once, just about banging my head on a bookshelf. (Business idea: meditation helmets.)

I read a knee-high stack of meditation books. I was doing all different styles—Samatha, Vipassana. Eyes open, closed, halfmast. I chanted in Hindi, in English. ("Don't worry, be happy," one book recommended.) I paid attention to my breath as it entered my nostrils and filled my lungs. I bought a book called *8 Minute Meditation*. Eight minutes! You can get washboard abs and become a bodhisattva with the exact same daily time commitment.

I read one book that said the key to meditation is to remember it isn't passive. It's hard work. Aha! This shifted my whole paradigm. It's basically working on your brain like a muscle. Meditation is free weights for my prefrontal cortex. I'm going to be the Mr. Universe of brains.

It's all about maintaining focus. You focus on something— your breath, your mantra, a soft-boiled egg—and if your mind wanders, you yank it back. It's a death match between your focus and your brain's desire to go gallivanting.

I meditated like I was going into combat. I will squash extraneous thoughts! That lasted a week, until I realized that's too violent. That's not Zen. I'm being pathetically Western.

You have to "gently and without judgment" guide your thoughts back to your breath. If I'm going to go with a sports metaphor, I'll go with surfing, which seems appropriately Californian. The mind has plenty of churning whitecaps. But you just need to stay above them. You watch your thoughts pass by as if you're watching a boat glide in the distance. Oh, look, now

I'm thinking about how I'm older than Sherman McCoy, the Master of the Universe character in *The Bonfire of the Vanities*, and how ancient he seemed when I first read that book. Okay. Well, so be it. Now focus again on the breathing.

Nowadays, when my alarm chimes after half an hour of meditating, I emerge in one of two states. Either I'm calm, serene, and sharp-minded, and feel as if I've just taken a run around the reservoir, but without having to put on sneakers or sweat. Or else I'm calm, serene, and befuddled, as if my brain has been soaking in some thick clam chowder.

So is it working? Are my focusing muscles getting buff? As novice as my meditation skills are, it does seem to help me in real life, at least a little. When I'm sitting at my desk, I'm much more quick to notice when my attention starts to wander. Where you going? Get back here, you big lug. I firmly but kindly pull the leash back to, say, my article on Mike Huckabee for *Esquire*.

THOUGHT CONTROL

That's the key. I'm much more aware of what I'm thinking about. It's like I've created a lifeguard for my mind, always watching, scanning. I'm obsessed with metacognition.

Sometimes, I'll let my mind wander a bit. As long as it's wandering into an interesting territory, I'm all for it. The problem is, it usually wanders into the same old neighborhoods. It dwells on ridiculous and embarrassing fantasies, like this one: I wish I had been the subway hero—the guy who jumped onto the tracks and saved another passenger—so I could have used my exalted moral status to promote my Bible book.

That's when I force my brain back into the present. Focus on what's around you. Unitask.

I've realized something else, though: when you're in the moment, you can be in the moment in a good way or a bad way.

I read David Foster Wallace's commencement address to Kenyon College the other day. It's a brilliant speech. It's about what we decide to think about during everyday, mundane tasks—waiting in line at the grocery, sitting in traffic.

We can let our thoughts follow our brain's default mode—annoyance, pettiness, outrage, selfish fantasies. Or we can make a conscious choice to "exercise some control over how and what you think."

Instead of snarling at the guy in the Hummer who just cut you off in traffic, you can consider the possibility—however remote—that the Hummer "is maybe being driven by a father whose little child is hurt or sick in the seat next to him, and he's trying to rush to the hospital, and he's in a way bigger, more legitimate hurry than I am: it is actually *I* who am in *his* way."

Today I passed a woman on the street who's a mom in Jasper's class. I've passed her several times before, and I always try to catch her eye to say hi, and she always looks through me with an empty stare, like an Egyptian pharaoh's funerary mask. It drives me crazy.

But Wallace was right. I should make a conscious decision to jolt myself out of my brain's lazy tendency toward pettiness: maybe she's really shy, maybe her sister is going through an ugly divorce, maybe she's just nearsighted. That's the noble path of unitasking.

LAST DAY

It's my last day. The plan was to really hunker down and do a perfect day without multitasking. I stashed my BlackBerry on the top shelf of a closet. I did my morning meditation to pump up my focusing muscles.

And then, at 10 A.M., I blew it. I watched a Demetri Martin video while researching an *Esquire* article. I checked CNN. com at noon. I took a cell phone call while making my turkey sandwich, though I begged off after forty-five seconds, ashamed.

It's now five-thirty and I've just punched the clock. I walk to the living room, where Zane has just dumped all the pennies and nickels from his watermelon-shaped piggy bank onto our striped rug.

His mission is to pour out all the coins and put them back in. Then repeat. His brothers are working on an equally important task: taking DVDs out of a drawer and putting them back.

Zane invites me to collaborate with him on his project. "Help, Daddy!"

I clink a nickel in the slot.

"I'm here with my three sons, putting nickels in a watermelon bank."

I say this sentence out loud, per the Bill Murray Method. I have three sons. They are healthy. They get pleasure from putting coins in a slot. I am overwhelmed with gratitude. Maybe it's the lingering effects of cold medication, but I start to choke up. A real "Cat's in the Cradle" moment.

Just outside my brain, three thousand things bark for my attention. My book deadline. Worries about the death of journalism. The invoice to the German magazine I forgot to send. But I've put up a soundproof wall. I'm going to put nickels in this watermelon with my son—and that's all I'm going to do.

It is the perfect, undistracted ten minutes.

CODA

I've decided to try to write this coda without taking a break. And to raise the stakes, I'm doing an experiment within an experiment: I'm writing it on a typewriter, so I cannot be tempted by the evil Internet. I have to say, this is quite satisfying, seeing the words appear on an actual piece of paper. It's so direct. No waiting for a laser printout. it's like cooking dinner instead of ordering in. That's not a very good metaphor, but I can't delete. It's actually quite freeing. No turning back!

Huh. This isn't working. I'm not staying on task. This sensation of typewriting is far too interesting. Haven't done it in twenty years.

Back to multitasking. I'm still an addict, but I've taken it down from a three-pack-a-day habit to a half-dozen cigarettes a day. Addict is the right word. Because I know it's counterproductive and harmful to check my e-mail every two minutes, but I do it anyway. then I feel shameful and dirty about it.

I'm very thrown off by the way that this typewriter does not automatically capitalize the first letter of the word. I'm at my dad's office because none of my friends had typewriters, but his law firm still has one Panasonic electronic typewriter. I read somewhere—and I can't check the Internet to see where—that Nietzsche's writing changed significantly whe he went from longhand to the typewriter.

It went from being more flowing and discursive to more telegram-like, bulleted and epigrammatic.

Which brings up the question (look at that segue—thanks typewriter): During my month of unitasking, did my thinking change at all? I hope so. A little. I'm calmer. I have a sense that I'm in charge of my brain more often, that it's not a slave to the blips and bleeps that pop up outside. I shut my eyes during phone calls. I'm getting more work done, which is huge. There's a lot of overlap with the Rationality Project and the George Washington project. The key is self-mastery. I've got control of my brain's steering wheel.

I don't think I fully comprehended how distracted I was before this project. One example: You know Walter Kirn's Atlantic article that I quoted? I must have skimmed that article three times before writing my essay. But only when I finished my essay and looked back at Kirn's for fact checking did I notice something unsettling. Kirn's essay has the same introduction as mine. Not the exact same. But similar. It's about him being distracted while driving. I must have been listening to music or watching the Mentalist the first few times I read it. my mind didn't even process what the first few paragraphs were about.

Speaking of which, a month after the end of the unitasker project, I had a chance to do something I hadn't done in two years: drive. We were visiting julie's dad in Sarasota, and Jasper desperately wanted to play miniature golf, his true passion.

Julie had to take care of the twins. So Julie very nervously decided I could drive jasper. It was a five-minute drive, no highways. But it was a tense five minutes. Hands on two and ten. No playing with the window or fiddling with the radio. "Daddy! Daddy!"

"Can't talk now," I responded. No time for pronouns, even.

We did get there safely. I can drive, as long as there is silence and the highway is straight and there are no flashing billboards to distract me.

$$Fame \leq Ego\,(x)^3$$

$$Zen + Focus = Productivity^2$$

$$\sqrt{Brain \cdot Caveman} = \frac{1}{x}$$

$$\frac{Outsourcing^8 + marriage}{12,000\ miles} = 9$$

$$x = \frac{Nudity + Public}{Dignity}$$

$$\sqrt{\frac{Nudity + Public}{Dignity}}$$

$$(Geo.\ Wash. - Wig)\,Me = x$$

$$\frac{Dating + Beauty}{x\,(Cyrano)} \neq Love$$

$$\int_b^a \frac{husband}{(wife)\,power}$$

$$(wife)\,power^3 = x$$

$$\frac{Reason - Emotion}{Behavior} = Insanity$$

$$Truth^n - filter = Chaos$$

A key member of my outsourcing team, Honey K. Balani.

Another indispensable outsourcer, Asha Sarella.

Chapter Two

My Outsourced Life

I really shouldn't have to write this piece myself. I mean, why am I the one stuck in front of a computer terminal? All this tedious pecking out of words on my laptop. Nouns, verbs, adjectives, *prepositions*. Sheesh. What a pain in my butt. Can't someone else do it? Can't I delegate this to one of my new assistants and spend my day kicking back on a chaise longue, Sam Adams in hand, admiring Evangeline Lilly's navel on my TV? What about having Asha write it? Or Sunder, Vivek, or Mr. Naveen? Or best of all, my sweet, sweet Honey? Pretty much anyone on my over-seas staff will do. Or maybe not. Maybe that's one of the lessons of these jarring and curiously enlightening four weeks. Dammit. I guess I'll have to write about the *lessons,* too. Okay, on with it. Here you go. As my team might say, thanking you in advance for reading this story.

It began a month ago. I was midway through *The World Is Flat,* the best seller by Tom Friedman. I like Friedman, despite his puzzling decision to wear a mustache. His book is all about how outsourcing to India and China is not just for tech support and carmakers but is poised to transform every industry in America, from law to banking to accounting. CEOs are chop-ping up projects and sending the lower-end tasks to strangers in cubicles ten time zones away. And it's only going to snowball; America has not yet begun to outsource.

I don't have a corporation; I don't even have an up-to-date business card. I'm a writer and editor working from home, usually in my boxer shorts or, if I'm feeling formal, my penguin-themed pajama bottoms. Then again, I think, why should Fortune 500 firms have all the fun? Why can't I join in on the biggest business trend of the new century? Why can't I outsource my low-end tasks? Why can't I outsource my life?

The next day I e-mail Brickwork, one of the companies Friedman mentions in his book. Brickwork—based in Bangalore, India—offers "remote executive assistants," mostly to financial firms and health-care companies that want data processed. I explain that I'd like to hire someone to help with tasks related to my job at *Esquire* magazine—doing research, formatting memos, things like that. The company's CEO, Vivek Kulkarni, responds: "It would be a great pleasure to be talking to a person of your stature."

Already I'm liking this. I've never had stature before. In America, I barely command respect from a Bennigan's maître d', so it's nice to know that in India I have stature.

A couple of days later, I get an e-mail from my new "remote executive assistant."

Dear Jacobs,

My name is Honey K. Balani. I would be assisting you in your editorial and personal job. . . . I would try to adapt myself as per your requirements that would lead to desired satisfaction.

Desired satisfaction. This is great. Back when I worked at an office, I had assistants, but there was never any talk of desired satisfaction. In fact, if anyone ever used the phrase "desired satisfaction," we'd all end up in a solemn meeting with HR. And I won't even comment on the name Honey except to say that, real or not, it sure carries Anaïs Nin undertones.

Oh, did I mention that Vivek sent me a JPEG of Honey? She's wearing a white sleeveless shirt and has full lips, long hair, skin the color of her first name. She looks a bit like an Indian Eva Longoria. I can't stop staring at her left eyebrow, which is ever so slightly cocked. Is she flirting with me?

I go out to dinner with my friend Misha, who grew up in India, founded a software firm, and subsequently became nauseatingly rich. I tell him about Operation Outsource. "You should call Your Man in India," he says. Misha explains that this is a company for Indian businessmen who have moved overseas but who still have parents back in New Delhi or Mumbai. YMII is their overseas concierge service—it buys movie tickets and cell phones and other sundries for the abandoned moms.

Perfect. This could kick my outsourcing up to a new level. I can have a nice, clean division of labor: Honey will take care of my business affairs, and YMII can attend to my personal life—pay my bills, make vacation reservations, buy stuff online. Happily, YMII likes the idea, and just like that the support team at Jacobs Inc. has doubled. And so far, I'm not going broke: I'm paying $1,000 for a month of eight-hour days from Honey (Brickwork gave me a half-off deal) and $400 for a month of four-hour days from Your Man in India.

To pay for YMII, I send my MasterCard number in an e-mail. The company's CEO, Sunder P., replies with a gentle but stern note: "In your own interests, and for security purposes, we advise you not to send credit-card information through e-mail. Now that it has been sent, there is nothing much we can do about it and we confirm safe receipt."

Damn. I know what he's thinking: How the hell did these idiots ever become a superpower?

Honey has completed her first project for me: research on the person *Esquire* has chosen as the Sexiest Woman Alive. I've been assigned to write a profile of this woman, and I really don't want to have to slog through all the heavy-breathing fan websites about her. When I open Honey's file, I have this reaction: America is screwed. There are charts. There are section headers. There is a well-organized breakdown of her pets, measurements, and favorite foods (e.g., swordfish). If all Bangalorians are like Honey, I pity Americans about to graduate college. They're up against a hungry, polite, Excel-proficient Indian army. Put it this way: Honey ends her e-mails with "Right time for right action, starts now!" Your average American assistant believes the "right time for right action" starts after a Starbucks venti latte and a discussion of last night's *Amazing Race 8*.

Meanwhile, I get an introductory e-mail from my personal-life outsourcer. Her name is Asha. Even though the firm is called Your Man in India, I've been assigned another woman. Hmm. I suspect these outsourcers figure I'm a randy men's magazine editor who enjoys bossing around the ladies. I e-mail Asha a list of books I want her to order online and a birthday gift I'd like her to buy my wife, Julie—a silicone pot holder. (Romantic, no?) Both go smoothly.

In fact, in the next few days, I outsource a whole mess of online errands to Asha: paying my bills, getting stuff from Drugstore.com, finding my son a Tickle Me Elmo. (Actually, the store was out of Tickle Me Elmos, so Asha bought a Chicken Dancer Elmo—good decision.) I had her call AT&T to ask about my cell phone plan. I'm just guessing, but I bet her call was routed from Bangalore to New Jersey and then back to an AT&T employee in Bangalore, which makes me happy for some reason.

Every day Asha attaches an Excel chart listing the status of my many tasks. The system is working—not counting the hitch in the drugstore order: Instead of wax paper, we get wax-strip mustache removers for ladies. My wife is insulted.

It's the fourth morning of my new, farmed-out life, and when I flip on my computer, my e-mail in-box is already filled with updates from my overseas aides. It's a strange feeling having people work for you while you sleep. Strange, but great. I'm not wasting time while I drool on my pillow; things are getting done.

As on every morning at eight-thirty, I get a call from Honey. "Good morning, Jacobs." Her accent is noticeable but not too thick, Americanized by years of voice training. She's the single most upbeat person I've ever encountered. Whatever soul-deadening chore I give her, she says, "That would indeed be interesting" or "Thank you for bestowing this important task." I have a feeling that if I asked her to count the number of semi-colons in the Senate energy bill, she would be grateful for such a fascinating project.

Every call ends the same way: I thank her, and she replies, "You are always welcome, Jacobs." I'm starting to like her a lot.

One task for which Honey is thankful is e-mailing my colleagues. I've begun to refuse to communicate with them directly. Why should I? Honey can be my buffer from the unpleasant world of office politics. I'll be aloof and mysterious, like the pope or Willy Wonka. This morning, I ask Honey to pester my boss about an idea I sent him a few days ago: an article on modern gold prospectors.

> Mr. Granger,
>   Jacobs had mailed you about the idea of "gold prospecting." I am sure you would have received his mail on this. It would be great if you could invest your time and patience on giving thought about his plans. Do revert and let Jacobs know about your suggestions on the same. As you know that your decision would be accepted with utmost respect.
>   Jacobs is awaiting your response.
> Thanking you, Honey Balani

Another advantage to this strategy: My boss can't just e-mail a terse "No," as he might to me. Honey's finely crafted e-mails demand a polite, multisentence response. The balance of power has shifted.

It's Julie's birthday today, and I've kept Asha busy with celebration-related tasks. Picnic orders, reminder e-mails to Julie's friends, and so on. Asha is more distant than Honey. I now have a vague sense of who Honey is—she's a mere twenty years old, likes to go bowling and go-carting, wears sleeveless shirts—but Asha? Nothing. In my few phone calls with Asha, I've noticed that her accent is slightly more pronounced than Honey's and that she speaks sort of in a monotone, so I can't even tell if she likes me. Which makes me insecure. And I'm even more nervous about her boss, Sunder P. He's been monitoring Asha's orders and sent me a note that she "missed the point" and bungled a communication about a kitchenware item. He's tough. But then today, the YMII team up and sends Julie an unsolicited birthday e-card—with butterflies and a Robert Louis Stevenson quote. I feel much better. I shoot back a thank-you.

Sunder P. writes back:

> Looking at the things we have been ordering on behalf of you, Asha almost was feeling like being part of your household. So isn't it befitting that we wish your family and be part of your celebration. (Remotely . . . from 10,000 miles away.)

I tell him that we feel she's part of the family, too. I don't have the heart to inform him that Julie was kind of disappointed that I had asked Asha to call 1-800-FLOWERS. The roses and lilies looked fine to me, but apparently 1-800-FLOWERS is the McDonald's of florists, and she was expecting more Daniel Boulud.

I think I'm in love with Honey. How can I not be? She makes my mother look unsupportive. Every day I get showered with compliments, many involving capital letters: "awesome Editor" and "Family Man." When I confess I'm a bit tired, she tells me, "You need rest. . . . Do not to overexert yourself." It's constant positive feedback, like phone sex without the moaning.

Sometimes the relentless admiration makes me feel a little awkward, perhaps like a viceroy in the British East India Company. Another cucumber sandwich, Honey! And a Pimm's Cup while you're at it! But then she calls me "brilliant" and I forget my guilt.

Plus, Honey is my protector. Consider this: for some reason, the Colorado Tourism Board e-mails me all the time. (Most recently, they informed me about a festival in Colorado Springs featuring the world's most famous harlequin.) I request that

Honey gently ask them to stop with the press releases. Here's
what she sent:

> Dear All,
>
> Jacobs often receives mails from Colorado news, too often.
> They are definitely interesting topics. However, these topics are
> not suitable for "Esquire."
>
> Further, we do understand that you have taken a lot of initia-
> tives working on these articles and sending it to us. We under-
> stand. Unfortunately, these articles and mails are too time con-
> suming to be read.
>
> Currently, these mails are not serving right purpose for both of
> us. Thus, we request to stop sending these mails.
>
> We do not mean to demean your research work by this.
>
> We hope you understand too.
>
> Thanking you,
>
> Honey K B

That is the best rejection notice in journalism history. It's
exceedingly polite, but there's a little undercurrent of indigna-
tion. Honey seems almost outraged that Colorado would waste
the valuable time of Jacobs.

Along the same lines, Honey wrote a complaint letter to
American Airlines for me; the flight I recently took offered only
shrimp for dinner, a dish I don't eat. "Since it has caused such an
inconvenience, I demand reimbursement," she wrote. Don't mess with
Honey.

Incidentally, Honey and Asha don't know about each other.
I'm constantly worried about getting busted for my infidelities,
for my life of outsourcer bigamy. What if they run into each
other at the Bangalore hardware store? What if I call Asha
"Honey" and she thinks I'm hitting on her?

• • •

My father-in-law has come to town, which means a dinner filled with a series of increasingly excruciating puns. Asked whether he ever suffered gout, he replies, "No gout about it!"

Damn, do I wish I could outsource this dinner. Where's Honey? Where's Asha?

I've become addicted to outsourcing. I am desperate to delegate everything in my life but have to face the depressing reality that there are limits. I can't outsource those horrible twenty-five-minute StairMaster sessions. I can't outsource taking a pee. I can't outsource sex with Julie. Not that I dislike it, but we're trying to have another kid, which means a whole bunch of sex, and enough is enough, you know? It gets tiring. I can't outsource watering the ficus.

Still . . . every weekend, I place a dutiful call to my parents. It's a nice thing to do, I figure—but it's also a huge time vacuum. This weekend it's Mom and Dad's anniversary, so I can expect it to eat up even more of my day than usual. Mr. Naveen to the rescue. I e-mail Mr. Naveen—the YMII employee who will be on duty at the time—a few concerned-sounding questions and a couple of filial sound bites. Next day, I get this e-mail:

> I made an out bound call to Jacob's parents. They very happily received my call. I first introduced myself to them. Then I wished them Happy Anniversary they both told me thank you. . . . I asked them how is the weather in their place. They told me that it is pretty nice temperature here and the garden looks beautiful.

I won't reproduce the whole report, but apparently my mom's sprained foot has gotten better (though the rain does not help), and my dad's law practice is going along very well. As for me, I had a good week, apparently. This was highly successful outsourcing, saving me at least half an hour of sweaty-eared phone time.

My outsourcers now know an alarming amount about me—not just my schedule but my cholesterol, my infertility problems, my Social Security number, my passwords (including the one that is a particularly adolescent curse word). Sometimes I worry that I can't piss off my outsourcers or I'll end up with a twelve-thousand-dollar charge on my MasterCard bill from the Louis Vuitton in Anantapur.

In any case, the information imbalance is pretty huge. I know practically nothing about them. So I e-mail them both to request a minibiography.

Honey sends me a two-page file called Honey4U. She's a jazz and salsa dancer, loves *Friends,* reads Jeffrey Archer. She has a boyfriend. She works from 2 P.M. to 11 P.M. her time and has an hour-and-a-half commute at either end. She trains people in customer-handling skills and in how to lose their Indian accent. She likes broccoli, coriander, and orange juice.

Asha, as expected, is a little less prolix but still gives me some nuggets: She's also a salsa dancer, oddly enough. She used to do something called "value-based education through dance." She studied electrical engineering, got married in February to a guy in real estate. She works from 9:30 A.M. to 5:30 P.M. Bangalore time. She lives with her in-laws.

I've realized something: Asha and Honey never say no. I find myself testing them, asking them to perform increasingly bizarre tasks, inching toward abuse of power. Read the *New*

York Times for me. E-mail me a bunch of questions from *Who Wants to Be a Millionaire.* Watch some viral videos and send me a summary. The closest I got to a no was when I made the admittedly odd request that Asha play the card game hearts for me, since I was wasting too much time playing it myself on my PDA. Asha replied that she thought this was a "good idea" but that maybe she would do it after finishing the other projects.

Emboldened by Mr. Naveen's triumph with my parents, I decide to test the next logical relationship: my marriage. These arguments with my wife are killing me—partly because Julie is a much better debater than I am. Maybe Asha can do better:

> Hello Asha,
>
> My wife got annoyed at me because I forgot to get cash at the automatic bank machine. . . . I wonder if you could tell her that I love her, but gently remind her that she too forgets things—she has lost her wallet twice in the last month. And she forgot to buy nail clippers for Jasper.
> AJ

I can't tell you what a thrill I got from sending that note. It's pretty hard to get much more passive-aggressive than bickering with your wife via an e-mail from a subcontinent halfway around the world.

The next morning, Asha CC'd me on the e-mail she sent to Julie.

> Julie,
>
> Do understand your anger that I forgot to pick up the cash at the automatic machine. I have been forgetful and I am sorry about that.

But I guess that doesn't change the fact that I love you so much.

Love

AJ

P.S. This is Asha mailing on behalf of Mr. Jacobs.

As if that weren't enough, she also sent Julie an e-card. I click on it: two teddy bears embracing, with the words "Anytime you need a hug, I've got one for you. . . . I'm sorry."

Damn! My outsourcers are too friggin' nice! They kept the apology part but took out my little jabs. They are trying to save me from myself. They are superegoing my id. I feel castrated.

Julie, on the other hand, seems quite pleased: "That's nice, sweetie. I forgive you."

I shoot off another e-mail to Asha:

"Could you thank her for forgiving me for not getting cash? And tell her that I, in turn, forgive her for forgetting to tell me about the Central Park date with Shannon and David until I overheard her talking about it with a friend."

The next morning I get CC'd on another Asha e-mail to Julie.

Am happy you forgave me for not getting the cash. And I am glad to do the same about the Central Park date with Shannon and David.

It's human nature to forget. Perhaps, I could do better by having Asha put up a calendar and sending us reminders about these little things.

Love

AJ

Good. At least this time I got my little dig in. But Julie just brushes it off—it's hard to trump a hugging-teddy-bear apology note. Like it or not, those damn stuffed animals improved my marriage. Asha should take care of all my bickering; she's my better nature.

Meanwhile, Honey seems to be lavishing me with even more adulation these days. She tells me that she waits eagerly for my e-mails. I'm beginning to feel like David Koresh without the guitar or weapons stash. It's a little stressful. I'm forever afraid of disappointing her, of not being creative or brilliant enough to merit her acclaim. On the other hand, maybe she's just doing her job and actually despises my white imperialist ass.

At the least, I figure I can take advantage of the exaltation. I ask Honey to write an entry in Wikipedia about me and my book, *The Know-It-All*. It reads in part:

> A. J. Jacobs is a not so unheard of international figure, who can threaten the most au courant wizards with his knowledge. . . . [He] is a writer and editor of phenomenal grey matter.

Perfection.

Friedman quotes outsourcing advocates who argue that we should embrace it as an opportunity. If someone else is plugging away on the lower-end tasks, that frees Americans to work on higher-end creative projects. Makes sense. After all, Jacobs is the creative genius with phenomenal grey matter. The world is better off with me focused on the high end.

But lately, Honey has started sending me unsolicited ideas— and some of them are pretty good. Granted, there are a few clunkers in there, and the English sometimes needs to be decoded, like a rebus. But there are also some winners: Honey suggests *Esquire* conduct a survey on what women want men to wear. Could work.

The point is, she's got talent. If Honey is a guide, the Indian workforce can be just as innovative and aggressive as the American, so the "benefits" might not be so beneficial. We high-end types will be as vulnerable as assembly-line workers. (Friedman's other pro-outsourcing argument seems more persuasive—that free trade will open up the huge Chinese and Indian markets to American exports.)

Regardless, if I end up on a street corner with a WILL EDIT FOR FOOD sign, then at least I'll know that I've lost my job to decent, salsa-loving people like Honey and Asha.

Despite three weeks with my support team, I'm still stressed. Perhaps it's the fault of Chicken Dancer Elmo, whom my son loves to the point of dry humping, but who is driving me slowly insane. Whatever the reason, I figure it's time to conquer another frontier: outsourcing my inner life.

First, I try to delegate my therapy. My plan is to give Asha a list of my neuroses and a childhood anecdote or two, have her talk to my shrink for fifty minutes, then relay the advice. Smart, right? My shrink refused. Ethics or something. Fine. Instead I have Asha send me a meticulously researched memo on stress relief. It had a nice Indian flavor to it, with a couple of yogic postures and some visualization.

This was okay, but it didn't seem quite enough. I decided I needed to outsource my worry. For the last few weeks I've been tearing my hair out because a business deal is taking far too long to close. I asked Honey if she would be interested in tearing her hair out in my stead. Just for a few minutes a day. She thought it was a wonderful idea. "I will worry about this every day," she wrote. "Do not worry."

The outsourcing of my neuroses was one of the most suc-

cessful experiments of the month. Every time I started to rumi-
nate, I'd remind myself that Honey was already on the case, and
I'd relax. No joke—this alone was worth the thousand dollars.

I've outsourced my marriage and filial duties, but somehow
my son has gotten overlooked. It's time to delegate some parenting to the Jacobs support staff. Julie is out watching her childhood friend do a stand-up comedy gig, and I'm stuck alone with
Jasper. It's 7 P.M., Jasper's bedtime, but I've got to write some
semi-urgent e-mails. No time for hungry caterpillars or jumping
monkeys.

"Mr. Naveen? If I put you on speakerphone, would you be
willing to read to my son? Oh, anything. The newspaper's fine.
Yeah, just say his name once in a while. It's Jasper. Okay, I'm
going to put you on now. Okay, go ahead."

A pause. Then I hear Mr. Naveen's low but soothing voice:
*"Taiwan and Korea also are subscribing to new Indian funds in
their markets."* Jasper isn't crying. I'm tapping away on my
PowerBook. *"European Union . . . several potential investors
. . . parliament."* I glance at Jasper again; he seems perplexed
but curious. *"Aeronautical engineers and technicians."* Jasper
seems to like aeronautical engineers. *"Prospects of a strong domestic demand."* After three minutes, I start to feel guilt-ridden.
I've officially begun to abuse my power. Why didn't I just turn
on the Wiggles? Then again, Mr. Naveen's lilting voice is so
comforting; if there were bright-colored cartoons of strong domestic demand, this would be ideal.

Speaking of the Indian domestic economy, it's looking pretty
rosy. My team is good, cheap, and absurdly eager. They will do
anything short of violating the Geneva Conventions. And with
most of the tasks—online shopping, thank-you notes, research—
my crew saves minutes or even hours of my day. Admittedly, the
outsourcing of my life is sometimes counterproductive—an ill-

fated order of an eggplant dish from a nearby restaurant comes to mind. But overall, it's working. To me, it seems the future of outsourcing is as limitless as . . . blah, blah, blah.

You know what? I'm kind of bored writing this piece. I'm going into the other room to enjoy some *Entourage* on HBO. So I've asked Honey to finish up writing this article for me.

> Once, I was watching *I, Robot* with my wife and I thought Life would become so easy with a robot. Then, the next instant I thought not just a robot but more of a humanized robot. In the book *The World Is Flat*, the author wrote about an interesting job that could be outsourced to India, which provoked me to have a Remote Assistant. Though I have never seen Honey K. B., I speak to her almost everyday when she calls me. Though our communication is not visual, I still know that she is a reliable assistant. Our interactions that we have had through mails and telephonic conversation never made me feel that she is miles away from me. To conclude I would say I did not get a robot but yes a Human like me who can think and work for me.

Yes, America, we're cooked.

CODA

This is me again, A. J. Jacobs. That was one problem with the aftermath of this experiment—when people e-mailed me about the article, and I'd write them back, they were suspicious. "Is this A.J. or is this Asha?"

So just so you're sure: it's me.

The article had an unexpected impact when it came out in *Esquire* in 2005. I started to get inquiries from people who wanted to outsource their own lives. I referred them to Brickwork and Your Man in India. A few months later, and perhaps nudged along by the response to my article, both those companies started departments devoted to personal outsourcing. "Virtual assistants," they're called and there are now dozens of employees at each. It's a real business. In fact it's getting so big I've heard complaints from some readers that the Indian assistants are overloaded. The tasks take too long to complete, and the results are unimpressive.

I must confess I had mixed feelings about the whole thing. Yes, these companies usually provide a good service. But what if my experiment helped take jobs away from American assistants?

I was feeling really down about this, actually. Then, six months after the article came out, a man wrote me. He said he works in technology and had lost his job the previous year to outsourcing. He'd been looking for a new job to no avail. After he read my article, he decided to hire someone in India to look for a job for him. That's right: he outsourced his job hunt! And the beauty part is, it worked. The Indian outsourcer found him a new job within a week. So maybe there's hope for American ingenuity after all. I'm crossing my fingers, anyway.

I still have Asha on retainer. Or actually, Asha recently switched jobs. So I now have her colleague Sunayana on retainer. I pay a fee of ten dollars a month and an additional ten dollars an hour. I use them every couple of weeks to make rental car reservations or research, say, George Washington's marriage.

Asha meanwhile sends me Christmas cards and digital photos of her cute two-year-old son. Honey wrote an "Ask Honey" column for *Esquire* for a couple of months after the article came out. She's now getting her MBA in India.

One of the calls I got in the wake of the article was from a young man named Tim Ferriss. He said he was a first-time author trying to write a business book. Something about how to

make money running an herbal supplement company while not
working so hard. And he wondered if he could reprint large
chunks of my article on outsourcing. I said, sure. Why be a jerk
and say no? Why charge him? He'll probably sell a hundred cop-
ies. Cut to: Six months later. *The 4-Hour Workweek* by Tim
Ferriss hits number one on the *New York Times* best-seller list,
and Tim (whom I love) becomes a massive celebrity.

In short, I need to outsource my business decisions.

$$\text{Fame} \leq \text{Ego}(x)^3$$

$$\text{Zen} + \text{Focus} = \text{Productivity}^2$$

$$\sqrt{\text{Brain}} \cdot \text{Caveman} = \frac{1}{x}$$

$$\frac{\text{Outsourcing}^8 + \text{marriage}}{12,000 \text{ miles}} = 9$$

$$x = \frac{\text{Nudity} + \text{Public}}{\text{Dignity}}$$

$$\sqrt{\frac{\text{Nudity} + \text{Public}}{\text{Dignity}}}$$

$$(\text{Geo. Wash.} - \text{wig}) \, \text{He} = x$$

$$\frac{\text{Dating} + \text{Beauty}}{x(\text{Cyrano})} \neq \text{Love}$$

$$\int_b^a \frac{\text{husband}}{(\text{wife}) \, \text{power}}$$

$$(\text{wife}) \, \text{power}^3 = x$$

$$\frac{\text{Reason} - \text{Emotion}}{\text{Behavior}} = \text{Insanity}$$

$$\text{Truth}^n - \text{filter} = \text{Chaos}$$

The founder of Radical Honesty, Brad Blanton.

Chapter Three

I Think You're Fat

Here's the truth about why I'm writing this piece:

I want to fulfill my contract with my publisher. I want to avoid getting fired. I want all the attractive women I knew in high school and college to read it. I want them to be amazed and impressed and feel a vague regret over their decision not to have sex with me, and maybe if I get divorced or become a widower, I can have sex with them someday at a reunion. I want Hollywood to buy this piece and turn it into a movie, even though they kind of already made the movie ten years ago with Jim Carrey. I want to get congratulatory e-mails and job offers that I can politely decline. Or accept if they're really good. Then get a generous counteroffer from my boss.

To be totally honest, I was sorry I mentioned this idea to my editor about three seconds after I opened my mouth. Because I knew the experiment would be a pain in the butt to pull off. Dammit. But I didn't want to seem lazy, so here I am.

What I mentioned to my editor was this: a movement called Radical Honesty.

The movement was founded by a sixty-eight-year-old Virginia-based psychotherapist named Brad Blanton. He says everybody would be happier if we just stopped lying. Tell the truth, all the time. This would be radical enough—a world without fibs—but Blanton goes further. He says we should toss out the filters between our brains and our mouths. If you think it, say it. Confess to your boss your secret plans to start your own company. If you're having fantasies about your wife's sister, Blanton says to tell your wife and tell her sister. It's the only path to authentic relationships. It's the only way to smash through modernity's soul-deadening alienation. Oversharing? No such thing.

Yes. I know. One of the most idiotic ideas ever, right up there with Crystal Pepsi and spa retreats for AIG executives. Deceit makes our world go round. Without lies, marriages would crumble, workers would be fired, egos would be shattered, governments would collapse.

And yet . . . maybe there's something to it. Especially for me. I have a lying problem. Mine aren't big lies. They aren't lies like "I cannot recall that crucial meeting from two months ago, Senator." Mine are little lies. White lies. Half-truths. The kind we all tell. But I tell dozens of them every day. "Yes, let's definitely get together soon." "I'd love to, but I have a touch of the stomach flu." "No, we can't buy a toy today—the toy store is closed." It's bad. Maybe a couple of weeks of truth-immersion therapy would do me good.

I e-mail Blanton to ask if I can come down to Virginia and get some pointers before embarking on my Radical Honesty experiment. He writes back: "I appreciate you for apparently having a real interest and hope you're not just doing a cutesy little superficial dipshit job like most journalists."

I'm already nervous. I better start off with a clean slate. I confess I lied to him in my first e-mail—that I haven't bought all his books yet. I was just trying to impress upon him that I was serious about his work. He writes back: "Thanks for your honesty in attempting to guess what your manipulative and self-protective motive must have been."

Blanton lives in a house he built himself, perched on a hill in the town of Stanley, Virginia, population 1,331. We're sitting on white chairs in a room with enormous windows and a crackling fireplace. He's swirling a glass of Maker's Mark bourbon and water and telling me why it's important to live with no lies.

"You'll have really bad times, you'll have really great times, but you'll contribute to other people because you haven't been dancing on eggshells your whole fucking life. It's a better life."

"Do you think it's ever okay to lie?" I ask.

"I advocate never lying in personal relationships. But if you have Anne Frank in your attic and a Nazi knocks on the door, lie. . . . I lie to any government official." (Blanton's politics are just this side of Noam Chomsky's.) "I lie to the IRS. I always take more deductions than are justified. I lie in golf. And in poker."

Blanton adjusts his crotch. I expected him to be a bully. Or maybe a New Age huckster with a bead necklace who sits cross-legged on the floor. He's neither. He's a former Texan with a big belly and a big laugh and a big voice. He's got a bushy head of gray hair and a twang that makes his *bye* sound like *bah*. He calls himself "white trash with a Ph.D." If you mixed DNA from Lyndon Johnson and Ken Kesey, and threw in the nonannoying parts of Dr. Phil, you might get Blanton.

He ran for Congress twice, with the novel promise that he'd be an honest politician. In 2004, he got a surprising 25 percent of the vote in his Virginia district as an independent. In 2006, the Democrats considered endorsing him but got skittish about his weeklong workshops, which involve a day of total nudity. They also weren't crazy that he's been married five times (currently to a Swedish flight attendant twenty-six years his junior). He ran again but withdrew when it became clear he was going to be crushed.

My interview with Blanton is unlike any other I've had in fifteen years as a writer. Usually, there's a fair amount of butt kissing and diplomacy. You approach the controversial stuff on tippy toes (the way Barbara Walters once asked Richard Gere about that *terrible, terrible* rumor). With Blanton, I can say anything that pops into my mind. In fact, it would be rude not to say it. I'd be insulting his life's work. It's my first taste of Radical Honesty, and it's liberating and exhilarating.

When Blanton rambles on about President Bush, I say, "You know, I stopped listening about a minute ago."

"Thanks for telling me," he says.

I tell him, "You look older than you do in the author photo for your book," and when he veers too far into therapyspeak, I say, "That just sounds like gobbledygook."

"Thanks," he replies. "That's fine."

Blanton has a temper—he threatened to "beat the shit" out of a newspaper editor during the campaign—but it hasn't flared tonight. The closest he comes to attacking me is when he says I am self-indulgent and *Esquire* is pretentious. Both true.

Blanton pours himself another bourbon and water. He's got a wad of chewing tobacco in his cheek, and when he spits into the fireplace, the flames crackle louder.

"My boss says you sound like a dick," I say.

"Tell your boss he's a dick," he says.

"I'm glad you picked your nose just now," I say. "Because it was funny and disgusting, and it'll make a good detail for the piece."

"That's fine. I'll pick my ass in a minute." Then he unleashes his deep Texan laugh: heh, heh, heh. (He also burps and farts throughout our conversation; he believes the one-cheek sneak is "a little deceitful.")

No topic is off-limits. "I've slept with more than five hundred women and about a half-dozen men," he tells me. "I've had a whole bunch of threesomes"—one of which involved a hermaphrodite prostitute equipped with dual organs.

What about animals?

Blanton thinks for a minute. "I let my dog lick my dick once."

If he hadn't devoted his life to Radical Honesty, I'd say he was, to use his own phrase, as full of crap as a Christmas turkey. But I don't think he is. I believe he's telling the truth. Which is a startling thing for a journalist to confront. Generally, I'm devoting 30 percent of my mental energy to figuring out what a source is lying about or hiding from me. Another 20 percent goes into scheming about how to unearth that buried truth. No need for that today.

"I was disappointed when I visited your office," I tell Blanton. (Earlier he had shown me a small, cluttered single-room office that serves as the Radical Honesty headquarters.) "I'm impressed by exteriors, so I would have been impressed by an office building in some city, not a room in Ass Crack, Virginia. For my essay, I want this to be a legitimate movement, not a fringe movement."

"What about a legitimate fringe movement?" asks Blanton, who has, by this time, had three bourbons.

Blanton's legitimate fringe movement is sizable but not huge. He's sold 175,000 books in eleven languages and has twenty-five trainers assisting in workshops and running practice groups around the country.

Now, my editor thinks I'm overreaching here and trying too

hard to justify this essay's existence, but I think society is speeding toward its own version of Radical Honesty. The truth of our lives is increasingly being exposed. Sometimes it's voluntary—think Facebook pages or transparent business deals. Sometimes it's involuntary—think Googleable political contributions or just ask Christian "Do Not Enter My Sightline" Bale. For better or worse, we may all soon be Brad Blantons. I need to be prepared. [Such bullshit.—*Ed.*]

I return to New York and immediately set about delaying my experiment. When you're with Blanton, you think, Yes, I can do this! The truth, the whole truth, nothing but the truth. But when I get back to bosses and fragile friendships, I continue my lying ways.

"How's Radical Honesty going?" my boss asks.

"It's okay," I lie. "A little slow."

A couple of weeks later, I finally get some inspiration from my friend's five-year-old daughter, Alison. We are in Central Park for a playdate. Out of nowhere, Alison looks at me evenly and says, "Your teeth are yellow because you drink coffee all day."

Damn. Now that's some Radical Honesty for you. Maybe I should be more like a five-year-old. An hour later, she shows me her new pet bug—a beetle of some sort that she has in her cupped hands.

"It's napping," she whispers.

I nudge the insect with my finger. It doesn't move. Should I play along? No. I should tell her the truth, like she told me about my teeth.

"It's not napping."

She looks confused.

"It's dead."

Alison runs to her father, dismayed. "Daddy, he just said a bad word."

I feel like a miscreant. I frightened a five-year-old, probably out of revenge for an insult about my oral hygiene. I postpone again—for a few more weeks. And then my boss tells me he needs the essay ASAP.

I start in again at dinner with my friend Brian. We are talking about his new living situation, and I decide to tell him the truth.

"You know, I forget your fiancée's name."

This is highly unacceptable—they've been together for years; I've met her several times.

"It's Jenny."

In his book, Blanton talks about the thrill of total candor, the Space Mountain–worthy adrenaline rush you get from breaking taboos. As he writes, "You learn to like the excitement of mild, ongoing risk taking." This I felt.

Luckily, Brian doesn't seem too pissed. So I decide to push my luck. "Yes, that's right. Jenny. Well, I resent you for not inviting me to your and Jenny's wedding. I don't want to go, since it's in Vermont, but I wanted to be invited."

"Well, I resent you for not being invited to your wedding."

"You weren't invited? Really? I thought I had."

"Nope."

"Sorry, man. That was a mistake."

A breakthrough! We are communicating! Blanton is right. Brian and I crushed some eggshells. We are not stoic, emotionless men. I'm enjoying this. A little bracing honesty can be a mood booster.

The next day, we get a visit from my wife's dad and stepmom.

"Did you get the birthday gift I sent you?" asks her stepmom.

"Uh-huh," I say.

She sent me a gift certificate to Saks Fifth Avenue.

"And? Did you like it?"

"Not really. I don't like gift certificates. It's like you're giving me an errand to run."

"Well, uh . . ."

Once again, I feel the thrill of inappropriate candor. And I feel something else, too. The paradoxical joy of being free from choice. I had no choice but to tell the truth. I didn't have to rack my brain figuring out how to hedge it, spin it, massage it.

"Just being honest." I shrug. Nice touch, I decide; helps take the edge off. She's got thick skin. She'll be okay. And I'll tell you this: I'll never get a damn gift certificate from her again.

I still tell plenty of lies every day, but by the end of the week I've slashed the total by at least 40 percent. Still, the giddiness is wearing off. A life of Radical Honesty is filled with a hundred confrontations every day. They're small, but relentless.

"Yes, I'll come to your office, but I resent you for making me travel."

"My boss said I should invite you to this meeting, although it wouldn't have occurred to me to do so."

"I have nothing else to say to you. I have run out of conversation."

My wife tells me a story about switching operating systems on her computer. In the middle, I have to go help our son with something, then I forget to come back.

"Do you want to hear the end of the story or not?" she asks.

"Well . . . is there a payoff?"

"Fuck you."

It would have been a lot easier to have kept my mouth closed and listened to her. It reminds me of an issue I raised with Blanton: Why make waves? "Ninety percent of the time I love my wife," I told him. "And ten percent of the time I hate her. Why should I hurt her feelings that ten percent of the time? Why not just wait until that phase passes and I return to the true feeling, which is that I love her?"

Blanton's response: "Because you're a manipulative, lying son of a bitch."

Maybe he's right. It's manipulative and patronizing to shut up and listen. But it's exhausting not to.

One other thing is also becoming apparent: There's a fine line between Radical Honesty and creepiness. Or actually no line at all. It's simple logic: Men think about sex every three minutes, as the scientists at *Redbook* remind us. If you speak whatever's on your mind, you'll be talking about sex every three minutes.

I have a business breakfast with an editor from Rachael Ray's magazine. As we're sitting together, I tell her that I remember what she wore the first time we met—a black shirt that revealed her shoulders in a provocative way. I say that I'd try to sleep with her if I were single. I confess to her that I just attempted (unsuccessfully) to look down her shirt during breakfast.

She smiles. Though I do notice she leans back farther in her seat.

The thing is, the separate cubbyholes of my personality are merging. Usually, there's a professional self, a home self, a friend self, a with-the-guys self. Now it's one big improper mess. Either this woman and I have taken a step forward in our relationship, or she'll never return my calls again.

When I get home, I keep the momentum going. I call a friend to say that I fantasize about his wife. (He says he likes my wife, too, and suggests a key party.)

I inform our nanny, Michelle, that "if my wife left me, I would ask you out on a date, because I think you are stunning."

She laughs. Nervously.

"I think that makes you uncomfortable, so I won't mention it again. It was just on my mind."

Now I've made my own skin crawl. I feel like I should just buy a trench coat and start lurking around subway platforms. Blanton says he doesn't believe sex talk in the workplace counts as sexual harassment—it's tight-assed society's fault if people can't handle the truth—but my nanny confession just feels like pure abuse of power.

All this lasciviousness might be more palatable if I were a single man. In fact, I have a theory: I think Blanton devised Radical Honesty partly as a way to pick up women. It's a brilliant strategy. The antithesis of mind games. Transparent mating.

And according to Blanton, it's effective. He tells me about a woman he once met on a Paris subway and asked out for tea. When they sat down, he said, "I didn't really want any tea; I was just trying to figure out a way to delay you so I could talk to you for a while, because I want to go to bed with you." They went to bed together. Or another seduction technique of his: "Wanna fuck?"

"That works?" I asked.

"Sometimes it works, sometimes it doesn't, but it's the creation of possibility."

I lied today. A retired man from New Hampshire—a friend of a friend—wrote some poems and sent them to me. His wife just died, and he's taken up poetry. He just wanted someone in publishing to read his work. A professional opinion.

I read them. I didn't like them much, but I wrote to him that I thought they were very good.

So I e-mail Blanton for the first time since our meeting and confess what I did. I write, "His wife just died, he doesn't have friends. He's kind of pathetic. I read his stuff, or skimmed it actually. I didn't like it. I thought it was boring and badly written. So I e-mailed a lie. I said I really like the poems and hope they get published. He wrote me back so excited and how it made his week and how he was about to give up on them but my e-mail gave him the stamina to keep trying."

I ask Blanton whether I made a mistake.

He responds curtly. I need to come to his eight-day workshop to "even begin to get what [Radical Honesty] is about." He says we need to meet in person.

Meet in person? Did he toss down so many bourbons I vanished from his memory? I tell him we did meet.

Blanton writes back testily that he remembers. But I still need to take a workshop (price tag: $2,800). His only advice on my quandary: "Send the man the e-mail you sent me about lying to him and ask him to call you when he gets it . . . and see what you learn."

Show him the e-mail? Are you kidding? What a hard-core bastard.

In his book, *Radical Honesty,* Blanton advises us to start sentences with the words "I resent you for" or "I appreciate you for." So I write him back.

I resent you for being so different in these e-mails than you were when we met. You were friendly and engaging and encouraging when we met. Now you seem to have turned judgmental and tough. I resent you for giving me the advice to break that old man's heart by telling him that his poems suck.

Blanton responds quickly. First, he doesn't like that I expressed my resentment by e-mail. I should have come to see him.
"What you don't seem to get yet, A.J., is that the reason for expressing
resentment directly and in person is so that you can experience in your body
the sensations that occur when you express the resentment, while at the
same time being in the presence of the person you resent, and so you can
stay with them until the sensations arise and recede and then get back to
neutral—which is what forgiveness is."

Second, he tells me that telling the old man the truth would
be compassionate, showing the "authentic caring underneath your
usual intellectual bullshit and overvaluing of your critical judgment. Your lie
is not useful to him. In fact, it is simply avoiding your responsibility as one
human being to another. That's okay. It happens all the time. It is not a
mortal sin. But don't bullshit yourself about it being kind."

He ends with this: "I don't want to spend a lot of time explaining
things to you for your cute little project of playing with telling the truth if you
don't have the balls to try it."

Condescending prick.

I know my e-mail to the old man was wrong. I shouldn't
have been so rah-rah effusive. But here I've hit the outer limit of
Radical Honesty, a hard wall. I can't trash the old man.

I try to understand Blanton's point about compassion. To
most of us, honesty often means cruelty. But to Blanton, honesty
and compassion are in sync. It's an intriguing way to look at the
world, but I just don't buy it in the case of the widower poet.
Screw Blanton. (By the way: I broke Radical Honesty and
changed the identifying details of the old-man story so as not to
humiliate him. Also, I've messed a bit with the timeline of events
to simplify things. Sorry.)

To compensate for my wimpiness, I decide to toughen up.
Which is probably the exact wrong thing to do. Today I'm getting a haircut, and my barber is telling me he doesn't want his

wife to get pregnant because she'll get too fat (a bit of Radical Honesty of his own), and I say, "You know, I'm tired. I have a cold. I don't want to talk anymore. I want to read."

"Okay," he says, wielding his scissors, "go ahead and read."

Later, I do the same thing with my in-laws when they're yapping on about preschools. "I'm bored," I announce. "I'll be back later." And with that, I leave the living room.

I tell Blanton, hoping for his approval. Did anything come of it? he asks. Any discussions and insights? Hmm.

He's right. If you're going to be a schmuck, at least you should find some redeeming quality in it. Blanton's a master of this. One of his tricks is to say things with such glee and enthusiasm, it's hard to get too pissed. "You may be a petty asshole," he says, "but at least you're not a secret petty asshole." Then he'll laugh.

I have yet to learn that trick myself. Consider how I handled this scene at a diner a couple of blocks from my apartment.

"Everything okay?" asked our server, an Asian man with tattoos.

"Yeah, except for the coffee. I always have to order espresso here, because the espresso tastes like regular coffee. The regular coffee here is terrible. Can't you guys make stronger coffee?"

The waiter said no and walked away. My friend looked at me. "I'm embarrassed for you," he said. "And I'm embarrassed to be around you."

"I know. Me, too." I felt like a Hollywood producer who parks in handicapped spots. I ask Blanton what I should have done.

"You should have said, 'This coffee tastes like shit!'" he says, cackling.

· · ·

I will say this: One of the best parts of Radical Honesty is that I'm saving a whole lot of time. It's a cut-to-the-chase way to live. At work, I've been waiting for my boss to reply to a memo for ten days. So I write him: "I'm annoyed that you didn't respond to our memo earlier. But at the same time, I'm relieved, because then if we don't nail one of the things you want, we can blame any delays on your lack of response."

Pressing SEND makes me nervous—but the e-mail works. My boss responds: "I will endeavor to respond by tomorrow. Been gone from N.Y. for two weeks." It is borderline apologetic. I can push my power with my boss further than I thought.

Later, a friend of a friend wants to meet for a meal. I tell him I don't like leaving my house. "I agree to meet some people for lunch because I fear hurting their feelings if I don't. And in this terrifying age where everyone has a blog, I don't want to offend people, because then they'd write on their blogs what an asshole I am, and it would turn up in every Google search for the rest of my life."

He writes back: "Normally, I don't really like meeting editors anyway. Makes me ill to think about it, because I'm afraid of coming off like the idiot that, deep down, I suspect I am."

That's one thing I've noticed: when I am radically honest, people become radically honest themselves. I feel my resentment fade away. I like this guy. We have a good meeting.

In fact, all my relationships can take a whole lot more truth than I expected. Consider this one: For years, I've had a chronic problem where I refer to my wife, Julie, by my sister's name, Beryl. I always catch myself midway through and pretend it didn't happen. I've never confessed to Julie. Why should I? It either means that I'm sexually attracted to my sister, which is not good, or that I think of my wife as my sister, also not good.

But today, in the kitchen, when I have my standard mental sister-wife mix-up, I decide to tell Julie about it.

"That's strange," she says.

We talk about it. I feel unburdened, closer to my wife now that we share this quirky, slightly disturbing knowledge. I realize that by keeping it secret, I had given it way too much weight. I hope she feels the same way.

I call up Blanton one last time, to get his honest opinion about how I've done.

"I'm finishing my experiment," I say.

"You going to start lying again?" he asks.

"Hell yeah."

"Oh, shit. It didn't work."

"But I'm going to lie less than I did before."

I tell him about my confession to Julie that I sometimes want to call her Beryl. "No big deal," says Blanton. "People in other cultures have sex with their sisters all the time."

I bring up the episode about telling the editor from Rachael Ray's magazine that I tried to look down her shirt, but he sounds disappointed. "Did you tell your wife?" he asks. "That's the good part."

I confess I didn't tell Julie about the cleavage incident, but I did tell my wife that I was bored and didn't want to hear the end of her story about fixing her computer. Blanton asks how she responded.

"She said, 'Fuck you.' "

"That's good!" Blanton says. "I like that. That's communicating."

CODA

Here's my radically honest opinion of my piece on Radical Honesty: I like some parts—especially the outrageous quotes from Blanton. And I think the intro works—though, frankly, I borrowed the idea (okay, swiped it) from Blanton himself. His book has a section called "The Truth About Why I Am Writing This Book," where he says "I want to become famous. . . . I want to get rich. . . . I want to be like Jesus."

But overall, my attempts at Radical Honesty could have been more hard-core. If I'd removed my filter in every single situation—instead of 90 percent of the time—I probably would have gotten beaten up, fired, and divorced. Then Blanton could never accuse me of "a superficial dipshit job." Then again, I might not have lived to write this piece.

I will say this: When you write an essay about Radical Honesty, you're asking for trouble. This came out in *Esquire* in 2007. Most of the feedback was positive (that's the truth), but I also got plenty of e-mails that said I suck. Or more precisely, I "suuuuuck." And my friends wrote me notes with subject lines like "Try standing up straight once in a while."

I had to do some apologizing post-piece, as you might imagine. I apologized to the woman whose cleavage I checked out. And to Julie's parents. And to the poor *Esquire* intern who transcribed the tapes—not just because of Brad Blanton's obscenities, but because I forgot to turn off my tape recorder when I went to pee. Three times. Sorry again, Meryl.

I knew I'd have to apologize. Since I'm laying it all out there, I'll confess that my motive for doing the experiment wasn't 100 percent pure. There was a devious aspect to Radical Honesty that attracted me. Here was a way to confront people without repercussions. Or with fewer repercussions, anyway. I could defend myself by saying, "Hey, I'm just doing my job, people. It's the project." Then say sorry later.

I got to tell my mom that I hate the smoked turkey she serves at her holiday party. I got to tell some old college acquaintances of Julie's that no, I'm afraid I do *not* want to have a playdate with them, since I rarely get to see my closest friends.

I still practice Radical Honesty—though only in certain situations. Call it Sustainable Radical Honesty. I'm especially fond of Radical Honesty about my own flaws and mistakes. I love the liberating feeling. No desperate scrambles to come up with excuses. No searching my memory banks to figure out what I told Peter versus Paul. It's all out there. Yeah, I screwed up.

I've also learned my relationships can tolerate a lot more Radical Honesty than I thought. If I just don't feel up to having lunch with a friend, I don't say my grandfather's in town for a special visit and I have to go on the Circle Line. I just say the truth. I don't feel like it. I've got three kids hopped up on high-fructose corn syrup and I need to take a nap.

But Radical Honesty about other people's flaws—that I can't do. I'm still a pathological white liar. Blanton thinks it's false compassion. I think it can be real compassion—especially if your wife asks you about her necklace on the way to the party, long after she can change it.

And after experiments with rationality and civility (see chapters 5 and 6), I've come to appreciate the filter between the brain and mouth. Words can be dangerous. Once they're out in the atmosphere, they can become self-fulfilling prophecies. You say out loud that your wife's friend is boring, then next time you see her, you perceive her as more boring.

Another confession: Since the article came out, the Radical Honesty concept has seeped out into the culture a bit more—and it kind of annoys me. A minor character on the Fox cop drama

Lie to Me is a Radical Honesty practitioner. When I first saw the show, I said, where's my credit? Where's my cut? Like I came up with the concept or something. Deluded, greedy bastard I am.

The Radical Honesty meme also caught on with single men, oddly enough. I met a Wall Street banker who said that, after reading the article, he and his friends had started using Radical Honesty as a pickup line. They'd go up to a woman in a bar and say, "I'm trying this new thing called Radical Honesty. And the honest truth is, I find you very attractive and would like to go home with you."

Nine times out of ten they'd get slapped in the face. But there was that one time . . .

And finally, regardless of what my editor thinks, I'm pretty convinced we'll all soon live in a radically honest world, for better or worse. It's going to be hard to keep secrets when every second of your life is Twittered and satellite-photographed and captured by tiny cameras. The truth will out.

$$\text{Fame} \leq \text{Ego}(x)^3$$

$$\frac{\text{Zen} + \text{Focus} = \text{Productivity}^2}{\sqrt{\text{Brain}} \cdot \text{Caveman}} = \frac{1}{x}$$

$$\frac{\text{Outsourcing}^8 + \text{marriage}}{12{,}000 \text{ miles}} = 9$$

$$x = \frac{\text{Nudity} + \text{Public}}{\text{Dignity}}$$

$$\sqrt{\frac{\text{Nudity} + \text{Public}}{\text{Dignity}}}$$

$$(\text{Geo. Wash.} - \text{wig}) \, \text{Me} = x$$

$$\frac{\text{Dating} + \text{Beauty}}{x(\text{Cyrano})} \neq \text{Love}$$

$$\int_b^a \frac{\text{husband}}{(\text{wife}) \text{power}}$$

$$(\text{wife}) \text{power}^3 = x$$

$$\frac{\text{Reason} - \text{Emotion}}{\text{Behavior}} = \text{Insanity}$$

$$\text{Truth}^n - \text{filter} = \text{Chaos}$$

Me as Noah Taylor.

Noah Taylor as Noah Taylor.

Chapter Four

240 Minutes of Fame

In my real life, I've had just the tiniest taste of what it's like to be famous. Three instances come to mind:

1. The book festival in Texas where I met my one and only rabid fan—a man who took off his sweater to reveal passages of my book scrawled on his T-shirt in Magic Marker. (Later, Israeli writer Etgar Keret would tell me that one of his fans got a chest tattoo of his book's cover, which made me feel small and inadequate.)

2. The time my mother-in-law called in a tizzy and said, "You're a clue in the *New York Times* crossword puzzle!" This was a dream come true. A bona fide mark of fame.

   "It's forty-eight down," she said.

   I grabbed the *Times* and opened to the puzzle. The clue was "Reads the encyclopedia from A to Z."

   The answer was N-E-R-D.

   Huh. Nerd. I would have preferred my actual name, but it was something. Just to be certain, I e-mailed the crossword editor, Will Shortz—whom I had once met at a crossword puzzle tournament—and asked if maybe I was the nerd in question; he said I wasn't consciously the inspiration, but that I might have been an unconscious factor. *Might have been an unconscious factor.* That's something, right? Good enough for me!

3. And finally, there was the awkward, Borscht Belt–like exchange with a passenger in the New York subway. "What do you know about Q?" he asked me.

Hmm. The Q train. "I think you can catch it on Fifty-seventh and Seventh."

He paused. "No, the letter Q. What do you know about the letter Q."

He had seen me on *Book TV* talking about how I read the encyclopedia, and thought it'd be fun to quiz me about one of the volumes. I was so disoriented, I couldn't process it. I just don't get recognized in public.

As for actual fame, that's about it. I've published two books that sold moderately well, but they haven't made me famous. Not in the real hounded-by-paparazzi sense of the word. On a good day, I'm "somewhat noted in certain quarters."

But if actual fame has eluded me, I have gotten to experience an odd simulacrum of fame thanks to an immersion experiment. The result was, as they say during *Entertainment Tonight* interviews—*surreal.* And it also convinced me that lack of fame can be a good thing. Or so I've told myself, anyway.

This experiment was actually one of my first, back in 1997. Early in my career, I worked as a writer for *Entertainment Weekly* magazine. My job usually consisted of interviewing B-list TV celebrities, writing down the type of salad they were eating, assembling a few quotes, and passing it off as an article.

But not always. There were exceptions. My most memorable assignment came in January 1997. The indie movie *Shine* had recently been released to an orgy of critical praise. Maybe you remember it? It was based on the true story of Australian pianist David Helfgott, who suffered from schizophrenia.

The adult Helfgott was played brilliantly by a stammering, tic-afflicted Geoffrey Rush. But the younger Helfgott—the post-adolescent Helfgott—was played by an up-and-coming Australian actor named Noah Taylor.

As it turned out, I looked exactly like Noah Taylor. Or at least like his slightly older brother. We had the same thin face, the same gangly body, and the same-sized nose, which in polite circles is called "prominent."

Even more striking, though, is that Noah Taylor and I shared the same haircut and eyeglasses. For reasons I'm still puzzling out, in my mid-twenties I decided to let my hair grow down to my shoulders. This wasn't cool long hair, mind you. It was shapeless and stringy, like Ben Franklin or a meth addict. And the glasses? They were thick, black, and clunky. I suppose I was going for a retro intellectual vibe, something in the Allen Ginsberg area. What I got was Orville Redenbacher.

Julie has told me several times that if I'd asked her out during my meth-addicted-popcorn-king era, we would not be married today. She would have told me that she was getting over a relationship and/or life-threatening, still-contagious illness.

The only upside, if you can call it that: my status as Noah Taylor's doppelganger, whose character sported the same unconventional look. From the first weekend *Shine* opened, I'd hear it at least once a day: "Hey, you look like the guy from *Shine*."

I'd humbly nod my thanks. If I was feeling generous, I'd mime playing some piano keys.

My editors at *Entertainment Weekly* noticed the resemblance as well, and were determined to exploit it. Turned out the real Noah Taylor was skipping the Academy Awards—the film was nominated, he wasn't, and he'd decided to stay in Australia. So my bosses came up with a plan: send me to the Oscars undercover. As a star. "I want to know what it's like to *be* a celebrity," my editor told me. "Do they have a secret handshake? How does it feel to be recognized everywhere you go? Will you feel the urge to open a theme restaurant?" (This was the height of the theme restaurant frenzy, when everyone with a SAG card had his or her own eatery.)

A couple of days before the Oscars, I fly to L.A. I rent a tuxedo, get a limo on the magazine's dime, and adopt my version of a Melbourne accent—which, unfortunately, sounds exactly like the Lucky Charms leprechaun. It's the best I can do.

On the big night, the limousine picks me up, inches along the traffic-choked streets, and pulls up to the red carpet at the Shrine Auditorium. I start to open my car door, but the driver stops me. "Wait a minute," he says. He comes around and opens it for me. Oh yes. Of course.

My forehead is already damp with sweat. I'm worried the ruse won't work—I don't carry myself like a star. I'm too slump-shouldered, too self-conscious. But as soon as I step onto the red carpet and wave, hundreds of fans in the nearby bleachers roar.

It's been thirty seconds of my life as a celebrity impostor and already I've experienced more power than I've ever had in my life. It's positively Pavlovian. I move my hand, several hundred people shout. Move it again, they shout some more.

"*Shine* guy!" they scream. "Hey, *Shine* guy!" A few actually shout my/his name: "Noah! We love you!"

The red carpet is surprisingly long. It goes straight for a few yards, then makes a right turn and flows a block or two down to the Shrine doors, which are flanked by four enormous Oscar statuettes. The statues look, as essayist Stanley Elkin once wrote, like "sullen art deco Nazis."

The rope line is jammed with hundreds of journalists and photographers. The drill is the same year after year: The journalists are like dog trainers and the celebrities are a bunch of unruly, uncooperative fox terriers. "Noah! Noah! Over here! Come! C'mon! Sit! Do interview!"

I wave off most of the pleading press with mock humility.

"I don't want to take away from Geoffrey's big night," I shout to MTV's Chris Connelly. (Geoffrey Rush is nominated for an Oscar—and will go on to win later tonight.)

"But Geoffrey said your performance inspired him!" Chris shouts back from behind the barrier.

"Sorry, mate," I say.

I finally stop for an interview with a Norwegian TV show. I figure it was an appropriately obscure place to make my media debut.

"What will you do next?" the square-jawed Norseman asks.

"I want to do some big event movie with earthquakes and hurricanes," I say.

"Thank you. You were wonderful. I wish you luck."

As I break away from the Norwegian team and continue down the carpet, I hear a roar behind me. Claire Danes has emerged from her limo. All the cameras and microphones swivel toward Claire like a crowd watching Wimbledon. I am last minute's news. Fame is fleeting.

• • •

Luckily, more positive reinforcement awaits me inside. The lobby of the Shrine looks as though it hasn't been refurbished since it was built in 1926. It's got a faux Middle Eastern theme going on—lots of domed doorways and arabesque designs in the ceiling.

But you're not supposed to be looking at the design. Because there's Ed Norton! And Tim Robbins! And Joan Allen! I know it's obvious, but the density of celebrities is stunning and disorienting. This many famous people shouldn't be clustered in one place like that. It's not natural. It's like going to a wedding where you're the only guest and everyone else is a bride or groom.

I was told by a friend who works in Hollywood that you're not supposed to sit in your seat. That's for suckers. The real power players just mill around the lobby, congratulating each other and ordering vodka tonics at the bar.

So I mill around. And am swarmed. The attention is overwhelming. Dozens of people—producers, execs, agents, and seat fillers—jostle to get close to me. "Phenomenal." "I love you." "Big fan." And most common, "Love your work."

"Love your work" is the standard celebrity greeting. When you meet a widow, you say, "I'm sorry for your loss." When you meet a celebrity, you tell him how much you love his work, even if you think he's got the charisma of drywall. As an entertainment reporter, I'd said it many times. Brad Blanton would be appalled.

One man asks if I know that fellow Aussie Paul Hogan is a fan.

"Isn't that nice?" I reply.

My admirers are outraged I didn't get nominated. "You

were robbed!" says one. I agree, noting that I've been so bitter,
I've trashed eight hotel rooms. "Good for you!" he said.

Usually, though, when I'm praised, I just respond, "Thanks.
But I'm no hero. Just doing my job."

It's not a joke, really. Just some words to fill the space. But
it always elicits an appreciative whoop from the listener. Because when you're a celebrity, anything that emerges from your
mouth that vaguely resembles a joke is cause for gut-busting
laughter from everyone within earshot.

I've seen this phenomenon from the other side many times.
I saw it with alarming clarity when I spent an hour with the
most famous person I've ever met: Julia Roberts. I met her because, for a few months in the 1990s, I dated one of her many
assistants. Rachel worked in Julia's vanity production company, which didn't actually produce movies or anything, but
which occupied a beautiful loftlike office in Soho. Rachel's
main job, as she'd tell you herself, was to be responsible for
the office aquarium. It was home to some lovely tropical fish.
And it was probably the most tangible thing the production
company had successfully developed. Every few weeks, Julia
would announce that she planned to visit the New York office,
and Rachel would be sent into a frenzy of Windex-ing and filter
cleaning.

Anyway, Rachel was sweet enough to wangle me an invita-
tion to the premier for *My Best Friend's Wedding.* I'd be her plus
one. Julia Roberts was actually friendly and charming—she
gave me her famous smile, shook my hand, told me she loved
working with my girlfriend. But the night left me drained and
sad. Being around Julia's posse, especially during the ten-minute
limo ride from the office to the premiere, was an exercise in exhausting forced merriment. It was the same vibe as New Year's
Eve—*You will have fun!* (said in Colonel Klink accent).

A typical exchange:

Acolyte: "Have you had dinner yet, Julia?"

Julia: "No, I am starving! I could eat a horse!"

We all erupt in laughter. We laugh like the crowd at a Chris Rock concert. Like we all just sucked down a tank of nitrous oxide. Like my two-year-old son laughs when he's getting tickled on his belly till he's gasping for air. We look at each other in amazement. *Did you hear what she said? Marvelous! Imagine a person eating a horse! The very idea! A horse is so big!*

A couple of years later, I interviewed Conan O'Brien for *Entertainment Weekly*. He was talking about what it's like to be famous, and he brought up the braying phenomenon. Conan said he actually liked to test the limits of this. Sometimes, he said, he'd be walking through an airport, and someone would shout, "Hey Conan!"

And he'd reply with a string of nonsense syllables— "Squidleedoo!"

And they'd crack up, shaking their heads in wonder at his wit.

So it is with me at the Oscars.

"How are you?"

"Great, mate!" I answer.

I'm bathed in a cascade of laughter.

It's not just laughter, though. I amplify every emotion. One fortyish producer, with no provocation, takes me aside and tells me about how his father was disappointed he didn't go into the family business of making linings for sport coats. It is clear he's tormented by his long-ago decision. But I—Noah—would understand. Because in the movie, Noah's dad was overbearing. So thanks to a mirage of intimacy, Noah has become this man's tuxedo-clad confidant. I listen and nod attentively. I tell him his dad must be proud of him. He seems relieved.

I continue squeezing my way through the crowd.

"Noah! Over here! Sign this! Sign this!"

I scribble the crowd-pleasing motto "Shine on!"

By the way, I never actually signed "Noah Taylor." I didn't even say "Hello, I'm Noah Taylor." People just assumed I was him, and I never corrected them. At the time, this somehow seemed more ethical than calling myself "Noah Taylor." Now I'm not so sure.

"Noah, just a word if you would!" "Noah, can I have my photo with you?" A lot of celebrity life consists of saying no. Or more precisely, having someone say no for you.

I know it's hard to feel sorry for celebrities, but I can see how these constant little requests can get irritating. I can see how you can get hardened.

A quick detour on the topic of celebrity requests. During my tenure at *Entertainment Weekly*, my night at the Oscars was the most bizarre experience—but it was followed closely by the time I stepped over a line and asked a celebrity for a favor.

This one happened when I was assigned an article on *Sex and the City*.

At this point, I had been dating Julie for a few months, and we both knew we were on the marriage track. I just needed to make it official by popping the question. I strongly suspected Julie would want a creative proposal. One hint came when she told me, "I want a creative proposal."

Julie has been a fan of *Sex and the City* from the time Carrie Bradshaw made her very first racy pun. (I believe it was something about "rising to the occasion." But I could be wrong.)

I called the *Sex and the City* publicist and popped the question: Would the actresses be willing to help me propose to my girlfriend? It wouldn't take more than two minutes of their time. I'd written a script and wanted to videotape each of the four actresses saying a line related to Julie. As in "I hear A. J. Jacobs wants to marry Julie Schoenberg. Which is strange. I thought A.J. was gay."

So the dialogue wasn't going to win any Peabodys. But it got the point across, and Julie would just be happy to hear her name pronounced by the *Sex* stars. The publicist called back the next day. The girls had signed off. They thought it was sweet. Yes! I was in.

I figured Julie would appreciate it. She loves her celebrities—but not in an unhealthy way. Julie has absolutely no interest in being famous. It just doesn't appeal to her. Nor does she want to be friends with celebrities. Her relationship to celebrity is like that of a visitor to the aquarium. She can enjoy watching the sea lions from afar, but she has no desire to climb onto a rock and start barking and diving for salmon herself. Interactions with famous people should be an occasional treat, like fudge or a pricey vacation. But she does love her treats, and I hoped to be able to provide her one.

I arrived at the set with my borrowed video camera. The show was spending the day filming at a beach in Brooklyn—which would be magically transformed into a posh Hamptons beach by the time it aired.

"They aren't quite ready for you," said the publicist.

The actresses were between scenes. I could interview them when filming was finished. About thirty yards down the beach, I spotted Sarah Jessica Parker (who played Carrie) talking to Kim Cattrall (the randy Samantha). A dozen greased-down extras in bikinis lounged on towels nearby.

"Do you want a pair of headphones?" the publicist asked me.

"Sure, thanks."

She handed me one from her stash. The headphones are

tuned to the actresses' mikes—it's so the director and crew can listen to the dialogue. But here's the thing: the mikes are rarely turned off. So you can often eavesdrop on whatever the actresses are saying between takes.

I put the headphones on and heard the following from Kim Cattrall:

"Why should I help this reporter with his goddamn proposal? It's not my job."

I pulled off the headphones. Oh man. This was not good. In fact, it could not be worse unless Kim Cattrall kicked me in the throat with her spiky Manolos.

"Um, I think I won't do the proposal stuff."

The publicist told me not to worry.

"Did you hear what she said?" I asked.

The publicist said that everyone but Kim Cattrall had signed off on the idea. It'd be fine.

I had a stress stomachache for the next four hours. But the publicist was right: the other three actresses recited their lines without complaint. Kristin Davis seemed to actually enjoy it, suggesting I do a few takes. Perhaps because she was the only single one at the time and so still had an untarnished view of marriage.

Kim Cattrall later apologized in her typically candid way: she explained she was "on the rag."

The next week, I spliced my footage into a tape of an upcoming episode. I slid it into my twentieth-century VCR and played it for Julie. Unfortunately, I chose the least romantic episode in the history of *Sex and the City,* one that features Miranda in stirrups at her OB/GYN for much of the show. It finally cut from Miranda's raised legs to Sarah Jessica Parker, who said, "My relationship with Mr. Big was going nowhere, and I had no possibility with A. J. Jacobs because he wants to marry Julie Schoenberg." To which Julie responded "What? . . . What's going on? . . . Oh my God . . . Is this my proposal? . . . But I'm wearing my ex-boyfriend's T-shirt!"

For some reason, that was the first thing that popped into Julie's brain. Then she hugged me. Then she demanded that I get down on my knees and propose like a proper gentleman. I couldn't delegate it all to the videocassette.

It worked out okay, but it was a humbling experience. I got schooled in my place in the caste system of fame. It's not the place of the Vaishyas to ask the Brahmins for favors.

The night of the Oscars, however, I'm on the other side. I'm the one getting requests. I'm the aristocracy. "Noah, come meet my friend!" "Noah, an autograph for my sister? She's a huge fan."

My friend Jessica Shaw—a fellow *Entertainment Weekly* reporter covering the event—has joined me at this point and is acting as my publicist: "We've got to keep moving, people," says Jessica, who's wearing a bright red dress. "Got to keep moving."

Things are going smoothly. Nothing can stop me. Across the lobby, I spot Geoffrey Rush, my co-star. Should I say hello? Yes, why not! I wait for him to finish his conversation, then approach.

"'Ello, Geoffrey!"

No response.

"It's me! 'Ow's tricks, mate?"

He looks at me. Alarm spreads over his face—the exact same expression my son had when he first saw the child-catcher in *Chitty Chitty Bang Bang*. I've gotten so cocky, I forgot that I don't exactly resemble Noah Taylor. I forgot Geoffrey Rush actually knows the *real* Noah Taylor.

Geoffrey glances around, hoping to lock eyes with a security guard. And then backs away without a word.

Shaken, I head back into the crowd for the deep-tissue ego massage of my adoring fans. "Congratulations, man." "Wow."

The (late) comedian Chris Farley grabs my shoulder as I walk by. "You were wonderful," he gushes, adding that he loved the piano playing. "Well," I confess, "that was done by a double."

I get a few more "I'm a fan of your work" remarks but it's almost over. Billy Crystal is about to crack his last joke. It's the usual four-hour triathlon for those watching at home, but I could have kept going for a day and a half.

The theater doors open and those of us in the lobby are engulfed by a throng of exiting actors and hangers-on. I'm pushed down a hallway. I accidentally step on the long train of the green dress worn by Jada Pinkett Smith, wife of Will Smith. The dress catches and she jerks back.

"Watch the dress! Watch the dress! Don't step on the dress!" Will Smith says. He isn't angry, just authoritative, the same way he handled the panicky crowds in *Independence Day*. He's even charismatic when he scolding you, that guy.

My friend Jessica and I are limoed to an after party. I give respectful nods to the Gold's Gym rats at the velvet ropes. I bask in the giddy welcome from publicists with headsets and clipboards.

Inside, more fans. I meet a screenwriter who tells me I *have* to go to Burning Man. I make sure to take time out and thank the cater waiters for bringing me my chicken satay. Noblesse oblige. Jessica and I linger for a while. But we both sense the night is over.

I go to my hotel room, undo my bow tie, and collapse on my bed, knowing that people like me, really like me. Or at least someone who closely resembles me.

For two days after the Oscars, I am on a high. I feel different, special. I get annoyed at the indignities of everyday life. Why am I waiting on line at the pharmacy? With all these . . . *people*. It's so . . . *ordinary* . . . Don't they know who I am?

I mean, I know, deep down, that all the gushing at the Oscars wasn't actually for me. But the intensity of the praise was such that it penetrated on some level. As with my stint as a hot woman, the lines between me and my subject have blurred.

Then the crash. The inevitable and depressing acceptance of my anonymity. You know what? I deserve to wait on line. I'm not special. Paul Hogan is not a fan of mine. In the span of three days, I go through a microwave version of the famous person's life arc: from a nobody to a god on earth to a has-been.

CODA

My night of fame put me in an altered state. I was drunk with fame, and not just buzzed, but seven-vodka-tonics drunk. The question is, Would I want to be drunk all the time?

I don't think so. I hope not.

Why? Because fame messes with your mind—even the fleeting version I had. In fact, if you believe a Cornell professor named Robert Millman, I might have been suffering from an honest-to-God mental disorder. Acquired Situational Narcissism. This is a multisyllabic way of saying that celebrities often become wankers. When you're famous, when everybody stares at you, flatters you, insulates you, you start to think you're the center of the world (a thought that has a grain of truth to it).

You gain the classic narcissism symptoms: lack of empathy, grandiose fantasies, rage, and excessive need for approval. It's why, as Stephen Sherrill writes in the *New York Times*, celebrities are so prone to throwing tantrums, getting married in the morning and divorced by the afternoon, demanding a private chef for their pet ocelot, and so on.

(Incidentally, not everyone buys the notion that people *become* more narcissistic as they gain fame. An opposing study argues that narcissists flock to show business in the first place. They arrive in Hollywood pre-deranged. Especially reality show stars. See note in back.)

You can see the quandary here. Fame makes people role models, whether they like it or not. It also probably makes them immature schmucks, if they weren't already. Therefore, our role models are immature schmucks. Which then creates a new generation of immature schmucks. Which is how we've arrived at the Kardashian sisters.

I don't know what the solution is. Term limits on celebrity? Five years as a movie star, and then you're shipped off to work at a T.G.I. Friday's? Should we boycott anyone famous who throws iPhones at their assistants? Should we do what the Romans did with their generals during the triumphal march? They put a slave behind the general to whisper in his ear that he was mortal, so his ego wouldn't expand.

Or maybe we should only support humble celebrities. Not all famous people are twisted monsters. Consider this: After the Oscars, I got a call from Noah Taylor's agent. Apparently Noah was shy and not into all the pageantry, so he was grateful I was there at the Oscars to represent him. He figured better me than him.

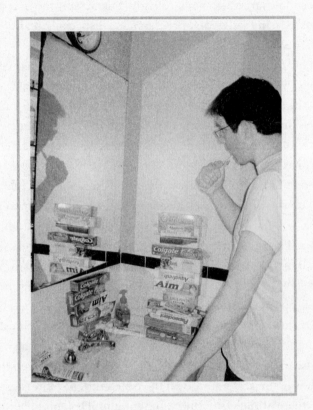

Part of my quest:
Find the most rational toothpaste on earth.

Chapter Five

The Rationality Project

My brain is deeply flawed. And no offense, but so is yours.

Your brain is not rational. It's packed with dozens of misleading biases. It's home to an alarming number of false assumptions and warped memories. It processes data all wrong and makes terrible decisions. Problem is, the brain didn't come to us fully formed from a lab at MIT. The brain is merely an ad hoc collection of half-assed solutions that have built up over millions of years of evolution. It's Scotch tape and bubble gum. If it were a car, it would not be a Porsche; it'd be a 1976 Dodge Dart with faulty brakes and a missing headlight.

As one scientist puts it, we've got Stone Age minds living in silicon-age bodies. Our brains were formed to deal with Paleolithic problems. When my brain gets scared, it causes a spike in adrenaline, which might have been helpful when facing a mastodon but is highly counterproductive when facing a snippy salesman at the Verizon outlet.

And yet we remain enamored of our ancient responses. These last few years have been a golden age for our most primal impulses. We recently had a president who spent eight years leading from his gut, and look where we are: a financial meltdown and a world filled with America haters. We've got Malcolm Gladwell's

Blink, a best seller with a subtle thesis that has unfortunately been boiled down to the pro-intuition message "Don't think, blink." It's given birth to a million stupid decisions.

I've had enough. I'm going to try to revamp my brain. Bring it into the modern era. I'm going to root out all the irrational biases and Darwinian anachronisms one by one and retrain my brain to be a perfectly rational machine. I will be the most logical man alive, unswayed by unconscious impulses. I'll use any means necessary—vigilance, repression, science. I'll also use duct tape, forty tubes of toothpaste, and a shroud over my cereal bowl. But I'm getting ahead of myself.

THE LAKE WOBEGON EFFECT

I came up with Project Rationality a couple of months ago. I'd always considered myself pretty logical, more Spock than Homer, more ego than id. But then I read a book called *Nudge,* by Richard Thaler and Cass Sunstein, which details the alarming number of built-in irrational quirks of the brain. Then I read another recent book called *Predictably Irrational.* Then another. And another. Turns out brain-bashing is an exploding genre, right up there with tomes about inspirational dogs and atheism.

If you read these books all in a row, you will feel like amputating your head. You learn your brain is programmed to be bigoted and confirm stereotypes. It's easily fooled by anecdotal evidence. Or a pretty face. Or a guy in a uniform. It's a master of rationalization. It believes what it hears. It overreacts. It's hopelessly incompetent at distinguishing fact from fiction. There are scores of "cognitive biases" identified by researchers (Wikipedia lists more than ninety of them).

When I told my brother-in-law, Eric, a behavioral economist at Columbia, about my plan to eliminate all cognitive errors from my brain for a month, he chuckled. He said I was suffering from the Lake Wobegon Effect: Our brains are delusively cocky. We all think we're better-looking, smarter, and more virtuous than we are. (It's named for Garrison Keillor's fictional town, where "all the children are above average.")

"You're vastly overestimating your abilities," he said.

THE AVAILABILITY FALLACY

I wake up on the first morning of Project Rationality. I've come armed. I've got a folded three-page list of cognitive errors, more than one hundred of them that I've cobbled together from books and Wikipedia. My method will be this: I'll analyze every activity throughout the day, see which blunder I'm committing, and try to correct it.

In the kitchen, I find Julie reading the *New York Times*. That's trouble right there. Journalism is an enemy of rationality.

What makes news? The unusual and the spectacular, which by their nature distort reality and pervert our decisions. You read headlines like 15 KILLED IN PLANE CRASH IN WYOMING. You don't read headlines like ANOTHER 2,000 DIED OF HEART DISEASE YESTERDAY. This leads to the Availability Fallacy. Our lazy mind gloms on to the most vivid, emotional examples. When we think of danger, we think of hideous plane crashes or acts of terrorism, even though boring old cars kill eighty-four times more people.

Today, there's an article about salmonella. Eight hundred people have gotten sick from salmonella, possibly from tainted tomatoes—which later will turn out not to be the case. I'm a

paranoid bastard, so I would normally purge our house of anything tomato related: the pint of cherry tomatoes, the ketchup
bottles, the *Esquire* cover of Andy Warhol in tomato soup. Salmonella would climb onto my list of Top Ten Worries.

Instead I take my first countermeasures. I ask my wife for
the newspaper, find a Sharpie, and scribble under the headline:
"Meanwhile, millions of people ate tomatoes and did NOT get
sick. But thousands did die from obesity."

"That's better," I tell my wife, handing it back to her.
There's something validating about writing it out. I explain that
every newspaper article should come with a reality-check box,
like cigarettes and their surgeon general's warnings. For now I'll
have to provide my own.

I go to the fridge and consider eating a cherry tomato to
spite the media. But that'd be falling for the Reactance Bias, the
unreasonable desire to do what others forbid you from doing.

UNIT BIAS

I do want to have breakfast, though. How to eat rationally? It's
a minefield. For starters, my list has something called "The Unit
Bias."

As humans, I've learned, we have an irrational urge to finish
everything on our plates. No doubt this served our Paleolithic
forefathers well when food was scarce and unreliable. But now
it just makes us a bunch of fat-asses.

I recently read about a brilliant experiment at the University
of Illinois a few years ago. They gave a group of test subjects
bowls of soup. What they didn't tell them was this: hidden tubes
underneath the table were constantly refilling the bowls. Guess
what? The subjects just kept on eating, long past when they were

full. If the scientists hadn't dragged them from the table, they might have exploded.

I need to eat less. I pour my MultiGrain Cheerios into a bowl, then cover the bowl with a napkin. I'm not going to let my brain see what's inside the bowl. That'd be too tempting. I'll just eat till I feel full. It's a time-consuming process trying to negotiate the spoon around the napkin. Which is probably a good thing, since it's healthier to eat slowly.

And yet I feel I have miles to go before I can say I ate a rational meal. Like yours, my brain is packed with food-related biases. People often choose the medium size at a restaurant even if the small would suffice—we have a fear of the extremes, so we go with the middle option. We find it logical to eat cows but not other mammals such as dogs or mice. Studies have shown we find things tastier if we pay more for them. Or if we eat them out of fancier containers. Later in the day, I eat microwaved chili off our wedding plates. It's delicious.

SOURCE AMNESIA

Here's one thing I'm learning: my brain is full of crap. I need a mental colonic.

It's the end of Day One, and I'm grappling with the startling number of myths, half-truths, and outright lies that clog my brain. It's not that I believe in ghosts. Or numerology. Or that Barack Obama secretly belongs to a mosque. My misconceptions are less obvious but just as false.

This struck me as I was brushing my hair. It sounds reasonable, and I suppose, for the first few seconds I get my hair into place, it is.

Problem is, I keep on brushing for another thirty seconds. I brush my hair till my scalp tingles. Why? Because someone—I think my mother—told me when I was about ten years old that you need to stimulate the scalp or you'll go bald. So that's what I've been doing for the last thirty years.

As soon as I uncover the almost-unconscious belief, it smells rotten, and about three minutes of Googling confirms it: it's a myth, about as effective as rubbing chicken manure on my head, another ancient remedy.

I call my mom to ask whether she was, in fact, the one who told me.

"That sounds like something I said," she says.

"Well, it's not true. It's a myth."

There's a pause. "Sorry."

"Well, I spent a lot of time brushing my hair because of that." (More than three total days of hair brushing, to be precise.)

"I'm not sure what to tell you except sorry."

Damn. Now I'm the bad guy in this scenario.

"Anyway," she says. "Why were you taking advice from me about baldness? You should have talked to your dad."

"I was ten!"

A huge chunk of my life has been wasted. Why? Because I'm the victim of two brain flaws. First, we place too much trust in authority. We follow the captain even if it's clear he's leading us right over Havasu Falls. It is hardwired into our brains. The second is just as insidious: Source Amnesia. We forget where we learned a fact. Facts are initially stored in a pinkie-shaped region called the hippocampus. But eventually the information shifts over to the cerebral cortex—where, as *Welcome to Your Brain* authors Sam Wang and Sandra Aamodt put it, it is "separated from the context in which it was originally learned. For example, you know the capital of California is Sacramento, but you probably don't remember how you learned it." A fact learned in the *Wall Street Journal* gains as much credulity as a "fact" learned from your cousin's barber.

And it gets worse. Even if we are told—clearly warned—that something is false or unsubstantiated, we often remember it later as gospel.

I need to root out these untruths. With a little research, I refute some of my more dubious beliefs: Shaving your hair does not make it grow back thicker, turning lights on and off does not waste more energy, sugar does not make you hyperactive. Despite what Mom said, I don't need to wear socks or slippers around the house for health reasons; you can't get a cold from cold feet.

Yet when I try to go shoeless around the house, it causes me such low-grade angst, I give up and put my Merrells back on. They are stuck deep, these myths. And I know there are dozens, hundreds, of other undiscovered falsehoods lurking in my neurons and warping my choices. But how do I identify them?

THE HALO EFFECT

It's Day Three and I'm pissed at the brain. It's not just flawed; it's superficial and cruel, like a cable TV pundit. This sunk in today when I was at Starbucks.

I bought a cappuccino and got back $1.35 in change. How much should I tip? Thirty-five cents or a dollar? I stuffed the dollar into the box and smiled at the barista.

As I poured my sugar, I realized I'd fallen for the Halo Effect. Terrible. One of the most evil biases on my little folded-up list. If a person is physically attractive, we unconsciously heap all sorts of wonderful, unrelated qualities onto them. Studies have shown we think attractive people are smarter than ugly people. We tend to hire them more often and promote them faster. We think they're more virtuous. Teachers treat attractive children better than their unfortunate-looking peers. In short, we judge a book by its cover.

And yes, the barista was really cute. A Maggie Gyllenhaal type with a moderate smattering of piercings. I know that was the reason I tipped her the buck. If she'd looked like Vladimir Putin, I would have gone with the thirty-five cents.

I unconsciously assumed she was a good person and deserved a dollar. I also, no doubt, unconsciously wanted to sleep with her and spread my DNA. (And assumed the sixty-five cents would help with that cause, naturally.)

The Halo Effect runs deep in our genes. It probably made sense to our hunter-gatherer ancestors. If someone had a misshapen face, there could be a greater chance he had an inherited disease. So you might want to avoid breeding with him. You want your offspring to have grade A genes.

I hate the Halo Effect. It's like Nature said, Hey, let's make life as unfair as possible. Let's load up the misery on one side and give all the happiness to the pretty people.

I call Richard Thaler, one of the authors of *Nudge*. (He's agreed to be my rationality guru.) "If you think about it," he says, "it's more rational to give the homely one a bigger tip. Some investment banker is going to propose to the pretty one soon and she won't be working at Starbucks."

The next day, before going to lunch with my wife at a local café, I take countermeasures. I put duct tape on the top half of each lens of my glasses. I'm blind from the horizon up. This way, I figure, I can still function, but I won't be able to see the waitress's face. I won't be swayed by her hotness. My wife reminds me I'm lucky to be married to her.

My plan works—for a bit. I can't see our waitress's face. But

I spend a lot of time listening to her voice—a bit husky, breathy—
to try to discern her hotness. Then I leave a big tip because I feel
like a schmuck for never making eye contact.

I call Thaler for a debriefing. "That was a good example of
what you don't want to do," he says. "You could have been hit
by a truck, first of all. Here's my advice: sit in the café, drink
your coffee, stare at the barista, then give your dollar to the
homely one."

CONFIRMATION BIAS

For someone who once deemed himself relatively rational,
I have an astounding number of superstitions. I suppose
"obsessive-compulsive rituals" sounds a bit better than "superstitions." Whatever they are, I've got so many, I can't count
them all.

After turning off the faucet, I touch it twice.

I never start or end a conversation with the word *you*.

Whenever I swallow, I must swallow in pairs.

And on and on. They take up a lot of mental bandwidth.

Superstitions, I learn, stem from the Confirmation Bias. The
faulty reasoning goes like this:

*I've swallowed in pairs for fifteen years, and I'm alive and
relatively okay.*

If I stop swallowing in pairs, who knows what will happen?

So I better keep on swallowing in pairs.

Highly irrational. Today, I've vowed to snap the superstition chains. I will have a superstition-free day. Perhaps even life.

I fetch my son, plop down on the couch, and start reading
him a story about a dangerously irresponsible zookeeper. Out of
habit, I swallow—the first big test. I suppress the urge to swallow again. A solo swallow, for the first time in two decades.

It feels odd. Where's the closure? Man, I want to swallow again. I feel like I sang "Happy birthday to—" and just stopped midsentence. I mentally tuck away the fact that I've swallowed a single time, so that when this experiment is over, I can swallow a second time to even things out. Not good.

A few minutes later, I walk by the hall mirror. Whenever I glance at my reflection, I start to contort my face into a yawnlike position, my lips obscuring my teeth. This yawning superstition started because I'm insecure about my overbite, so I hide it. The yawn makes me resemble an orangutan in estrus. I stop myself, relax my face. I'd forgotten about this quirk when I was making my list. These rituals are lurking everywhere.

The ritual-breaking has made me anxious. My heart rate has jumped. I'm hyperaware of everything going on, looking for any sign of catastrophe or disease.

"Everything okay?" I ask Julie.

"Uh, fine, thanks."

"Nothing bad has happened to you this morning?"

She shakes her head.

A couple of hours later, I catch the digital clock in our bedroom change from minute 13 to 14. So what? I don't need to stop and stare at the clock until it changes from 14 to 15 so that the 13 is washed out of my mind.

By the end of the day, I'm on a high. Why didn't I do this twenty years ago? Think of the time I could have saved.

I wake up the next morning, ready for another day of freedom. An hour into the day, I spill coffee all over my MacBook keyboard. Yeah, well, it happens. A few minutes later, Julie asks me if I've seen her earring. She's lost it somewhere. She looks upset—even more than lost-earring upset. Well, she says, a client of hers had just called and shouted some unreasonable demands. "She's a bulldozer," she says.

Then I get an angry e-mail about an essay I wrote. I'd committed a big mistake—I hadn't made it clear that I disguised the identities of everyone in the essay—and it made me look like an insensitive tool.

I knew this would happen. What kind of an idiot am I to tempt fate? This experiment is over.

THE MERE EXPOSURE EFFECT

It's a couple of days later. Maybe I've overreacted a bit. I'm sticking with my swallowing in pairs, but perhaps there's other irrational behavior I can fix. Like my toothpaste preference.

I've brushed with Crest pretty much every day for the past thirty years. (The exception: one night last year, I brushed my teeth with Preparation H. The reasons were several: a poorly lit hotel bathroom, lack of sleep, a couple of Rolling Rocks, and two identically sized tubes in my Dopp kit.)

Why Crest? I can't say for sure. No pro/con list was ever drawn up. Some friend of mine at Camp Powhatan in Maine used Crest. He was cool and had seemingly good dental hygiene. I started using Crest—and never stopped.

It's scary once you start to scrutinize it. Probably 90 percent of our life decisions are powered by the twin engines of inertia and laziness.

Psychologists call it the Mere Exposure Effect. The basic idea is, I like Crest because I'm accustomed to Crest.

That's not good enough. I need a fully rational toothpaste. I need, first, to expand my dental hygiene horizons. I go to the drugstore and buy a sample platter of forty tubes of toothpaste. (The cashier doesn't even bat an eye; I guess when your customers buy bungee cords and vats of K-Y Jelly in preparation for a Friday night, this isn't a big deal.)

I go home and spend eighty minutes brushing. Pepsodent Smooth Mint. Colgate Luminous Crystal Clean Mint. Aquafresh Extreme Clean Whitening Mint Experience. I never realized how much I hate mint. What a tongue-stinging, foul taste. It brings back bad memories of the green goo that goes with lamb chops. What kind of stranglehold do the mint growers have on toothpaste makers? Bite me, mint lobby. The occasional cinnamon paste tastes a bit better, I guess.

But toothpaste No. 27—this is a revelation. Tom's apricot toothpaste. It's fresh and clean-tasting, but not heavy-handed, and with just a hint of licorice. It's like something you'd eat at Chez Panisse. I might actually look forward to toothbrushing.

So that's a winner in taste. But what about the other factors? Whitening. Cavity-fighting power. Price. The dispenser. The ethics of the manufacturer.

I could spend days researching and testing this decision. I feel like Buridan's ass. This is a donkey in a philosophical parable: He's hungry and thirsty and standing equidistant between a bucket of water and a bucket of food. He dies deciding.

The Internet has dozens of articles on comparative toothpaste studies. I consult Consumersearch.com, which aggregates reviews from other consumer sites. "Colgate leads the pack," it reports. "Experts recommend Colgate Total most often." Okay. So maybe Colgate Total will be my pick.

But here's another key sentence: "Even the sites and publications which do make recommendations acknowledge that any approved toothpaste will benefit the consumer. Choices based on taste or consistency preferences are valid, and will not greatly affect oral health."

Okay, so taste it is. Apricot is the way to go. Then I look carefully at the apricot tube—there's no mention of ADA approval. I call the 800 number and find out approval is still "pending." Ugh. I call Thaler.

"I hate the taste of toothpaste," says Thaler. "If there's one that tastes like apricot, I'm there."

I promise to e-mail him the info.

"We don't want to make the mistake that only quantifiable things—like number of cavities—go into a rational decision," he says. "Rationality is all about trade-offs. Say I get a cavity once every decade. And with this toothpaste, I get a cavity once every nine years. The pleasure of the daily toothbrushing might make apricot the rational choice. Put it this way: if you choose the safest car even if it's ugly and no fun to drive, then it might not be rational."

That makes me feel better. Sort of. Now I'm worried I'll never find the line between rationality and rationalizing.

THE TEXAS SHARPSHOOTER FALLACY

Two weeks in, and I'm turning into a bit of a pompous ass, it seems. I can't resist pointing out other people's cognitive biases.

My aunt Kate, an Orthodox Jew, sent me a viral e-mail today titled "God's Pharmacy." It's about how the shapes of food contain clues from God about nutrition.

"A sliced carrot looks like the human eye . . . science now shows carrots greatly enhance blood flow to the eyes."

"A tomato has four chambers and is red . . . the heart has four chambers and is red. Research shows tomatoes are loaded with lycopene and are indeed pure heart and blood food."

And on it went, with walnuts connected to brains and rhubarb resembling bones.

I reply, "Thanks, Kate!" I thought I'd start out polite, at least.

"This seems like it's an example of the Texas Sharpshooter Fallacy." (This is a logical fallacy, as described on Wikipedia, in which information that has no relationship is interpreted or manipulated until it appears to have meaning. The name comes from a story about a Texan who fires several shots at the side of a barn, then paints a target centered on the hits and claims to be a sharpshooter.) "I'm not saying God doesn't exist, just that this food-shape idea is seriously flawed."

I press SEND. I try not to feel smug. It's just that these biases have given me a handy lens through which to view human thought. Simply being able to give a name—especially a cool one like Texas Sharpshooter—orders the chaos.

Kate replies that God designed the world in an infinitely subtle way to preserve our independence. So we must look deep to discover hidden truths.

I e-mail Kate again to say that the "God's Pharmacy" e-mail is related to another brain quirk. This one is called the Law of Similarity. If X and Y look similar, humans believe they are somehow related, whether they are or not.

This can be seen in my favorite experiment of all time: Psychologists asked students to eat a piece of fudge shaped like dog feces. The students couldn't do it—even though they knew rationally that it was just sugar, milk, butter, and cocoa. (This experiment, by the way, ruined my business plan for turd-shaped truffles.)

No response from Kate.

THE NARRATIVE FALLACY

I'm all cocky with Kate. But it's not like I'm in much better shape. Rationality is an elusive goal.

Today, my son Zane threw a monster tantrum. (I have three

sons now—my wife gave birth to twin boys soon after the Radical Honesty experiment.) Half an hour of flying arms and screaming (punctuated by his occasional pauses to look up and make sure we were watching his epic flailing). Julie blames all our kids' tantrums on lack of sleep. I blame them on lack of food. He's overtired. No, he's overhungry. Same debate every time. Rationally, I know we're both oversimplifying. There are probably a dozen factors. But we humans like to tell a story. X happened because of Y. The end.

Nassim Nicholas Taleb talks about this in his depressing but eye-opening book *The Black Swan*. When the newscasters report on the Dow dropping, they always have some explanation. Housing starts were slow, so the Dow dropped. IBM reported lower-than-expected profits, so the Dow dropped. Bernanke's taking goiter medication, so the Dow dropped. Truth is, they have no clue. The actual causes are way too complex. A thousand factors played into the drop.

The same goes for the opposite direction. We like to take a simple incident and think we can predict its effect far into the future. We see a butterfly flap its wings in Jersey, and we think we can figure out whether it's going to snow in Wyoming.

This I battle every day. Fatherhood has taken it to unhealthy extremes. As an overprotective dad, I analyze every little thing my kids do. I say to myself, "What will the consequence of that be in five minutes? In five years? In twenty years?"

Jasper got a DVD of the movie *Surf's Up* for his fourth birthday. It's about penguins who surf. My irrational thinking went like this:

Surfing is dangerous.

If he watches Surf's Up, *he might take up surfing later in life.*

If he takes up surfing, he might suffer a serious injury.

So I hid the DVD. Julie foraged around for it for several days before I fessed up.

"I think it might be in the closet with the winter coats," I said.

"Why might it be there?"

I knew the logic was flawed. My inner Tipper Gore had gone nuts. I was aware of that, and yet I still hid the DVD. I willfully ignored a hundred other variables: The joy Jasper might get from watching *Surf's Up*. The millions of *Surf's Up* viewers who won't end up surfers. The millions of surfers who don't end up in intensive care. I'm wasting a lot of mental energy.

Then again, believing you have control—even if that control is an illusion—does make people happier. One study found that oldsters in a retirement home were happier when they thought they were controlling the heat, even when they weren't. So maybe you have to balance two things: the unpleasant feeling I get from worrying about future surfing accidents versus the good feeling I get from at least trying to influence my kid's future.

And now I have just given myself a headache.

SPONTANEOUS TRAIT TRANSFERENCE

I've been struggling with a work dilemma. The problem is, I've become what is officially known as a "blurb whore."

Since I've written two books about going on unlikely quests (one about reading the encyclopedia, the other about living by the Bible), I'm now linked to the genre. So I'm getting sent a lot of manuscripts with titles like "Top Brass: One Man's Humble Quest to Master the Flügelhorn."

Unless I really dislike the book, I try to say something nice about it, even if it's to compliment the choice of typeface.

But now I've been asked to endorse a bunch of books that hit shelves at the exact same time as the paperback of my Bible book. And these books are about religion. Should I really be cannibalizing my own sales?

I think I'm going to have to be a jerk and say no. Which gives me a stomachache. Until I read about a cognitive bias called Spontaneous Trait Transference. This is a fascinating fallacy with huge implications.

Here's how author Gretchen Rubin, of Happiness-project .com, describes it:

> People will unintentionally associate what I say about the qualities of other people with my own qualities. So if I told Jean that Pat is arrogant, unconsciously Jean would associate that quality with me. On the other hand, if I said that Pat is brilliant or hilarious, I'd be linked to those qualities. What I say about other people sticks to me—even when I talk to someone who already knows me. So it behooves me to say only good things.

This has got to be the most wonderful brain quirk around. It's built-in biological karma. You trash-talk someone, it boomerangs back on you. You say kind things, you become a hero. So calling a book "ingenious" actually makes people think *I'm* ingenious. Being a blurb whore is good business.

Of course, I know, rationally, I could find good reasons why blurb whoring is terrible for business. But I don't want to. So I stop while I'm ahead.

THE MIRROR EFFECT

Julie and I made a trip to the grocery. Nowadays—three weeks into Project Rationality—I'm hyperaware of other people's attempts to take advantage of my brain. For instance, I know that groceries position the high-profit items at eye level, because we lazy humans are more likely to buy the first thing we see. Not me. I've started to shop with my knees bent and crouched down low, like a major league catcher, waddling through the aisles, a diminutive bargain hunter.

I know that grocery stores often pump out the artificial smell of baking bread throughout the day, because it makes customers hungrier and more likely to load up their carts. So I shop while breathing only through my mouth.

Julie laughs at me.

"You don't have to do that in our grocery store."

I take a sniff. She's right. Our local market smells like the penguin house at the Central Park Zoo, which doesn't do much for the appetite.

The point is, the human brain is easy prey for influencers. I should clarify, though: I've got no qualms about tricking the brain. The key is, the influence should be for the good, not to sell us more breadlike substances with high-fructose corn syrup.

I try to trick my own brain into being better. At home, I've put a mirror next to my computer screen. I did this because studies show people behave more virtuously when a mirror is present. They can see themselves sinning, and they stop. I swear it's cut down on the number of times I check media gossip websites.

And even better than mirrors—eyes. Studies show that people behave more ethically when there are pictures of eyes on the wall. You don't even need real eyes. Just pictures of eyes. People unconsciously think they're being watched and judged.

I've snipped out dozens of eyes from magazines—Sela Ward's eyes from a clothing ad, John Malkovich's from an interview—and taped them around the house. I put a stern-looking set of eyes (Lynne Cheney's) on the cabinet where the fruit snacks are kept. I taped a dozen pairs of eyes in the kids' room. Is it working? Hard to tell. My son Lucas hasn't thrown a tantrum about sharing his Hot Wheels jeep in a week. But I'd need a more rigorous study to be sure.

I do know this: Zane enjoys engaging in staring contests with the eyes. He'll get his face up real close and stare for several minutes, trying, I suppose, to make John Malkovich blink. So that keeps him out of trouble.

THE ENDOWMENT EFFECT

To get inspired, I've been watching Spock on YouTube and reading *Star Trek* scripts. Like this exchange:

> Bailey: I happen to have a human thing called an adrenaline gland.
> Spock: It does sound most inconvenient. . . . Have you considered having it removed?

It's a joke. But I actually think it's not a bad idea. At least for those of us who never go hiking and don't need to flee from grizzlies. I've become more and more wary of emotion. Scientists talk about System 1 and System 2. System 1 is the more ancient part of the brain and roughly corresponds to the "gut." System 2 is the more recent, evolutionarily speaking, and roughly corresponds to reason or the mind.

System 1 is Homer. System 2 is Spock. Some commentators have compared it to a monkey controlling a wild elephant. Gary Marcus, author of the book *Kluge*, puts it this way: System 2 is "deliberative" and reflective. It's not always rational, but at least it tries. System 1 isn't always irrational, but it's "shortsighted" and "ancestral."

I realize Project Rationality is my attempt to live completely under System 2 and override the unstable lizard brain that is System 1.

This is disorienting to other people. Humans crave melodrama. Julie got upset with me today for not getting upset enough. I had done something dumb. I'd left our son's stroller in the back of a cab. It was a cheapo stroller, but still.

"Well, that was a mistake," I said when we realized it. "I will try not to do that again." (I do notice I'm using fewer contractions. Getting too into this Spock character?)

"That's it?" she asked.

"What do you want?"

"You're so blasé."

"You want theatrics?"

"I want you to say something like 'Oh no, that's terrible. I can't believe I did that. I feel horrible.' "

I explained that I didn't feel that way. I felt annoyed at myself, and I vowed to try not to do it again. But I will probably forget other things in the future, so she should be prepared. In either case, throwing a hissy fit wouldn't get the stroller back nor help reform my behavior; it'd just create negative emotions. Plus, we overestimate the value of things we own—it's called the Endowment Effect.

My wife said our son needs to understand the value of objects.

I paused. "Point taken," I said. Our son is still a System 1 creature. "Next time, I will put on a show for our son."

My wife stomped out.

LAKE WOBEGON, PART 2

When I started this project, I thought I'd come to the conclusion that System 1 and System 2 are equally necessary. We need volcanic emotions as much as reasoned logic. But I've become more leery of System 1 every day. True, occasionally we need it. When we lose our balance and grab for the subway pole, that's instinct. We short-circuit the rational brain because there's no time for reason to get involved. But that's the exception. If I had to guess, I'd blame System 1 for 90 percent of wars and murders.

My ideal? A world of Spocks, but Spocks who are joyful and compassionate and life-loving. Spocks who brush with apricot toothpaste because it tastes delicious.

But I may have overestimated my ability to control System 1.

A week after my even-tempered stroller reaction, as my month comes to an end, I'm at a restaurant with my son Jasper, waiting to play foosball. Two European teenagers are playing. They're accomplished foosballers, I can tell. They spin the rods expertly, scoring quickly, zipping the game along. Until they get to the last ball.

At which point they decide it'd be fun to draw the game out as long as possible. They pass the foosball back and forth slowly and carefully between their offensive lines.

"When will it be our turn?" asks my son.

"Soon."

Two minutes go by. Five minutes. My son has asked the above question a half-dozen times by now.

"What's going on here?" I ask the teens.

"Vee are trying." They snicker—actually snicker. Then talk in German.

Ten minutes go by.

I know exactly what's happening in my brain as it's happening, and yet I feel like I can't stop it. My limbic system kicks in. My pulse triples.

"You are not trying. You are stalling."

"No, really. Vee are trying." More snickers.

My emotions have hijacked my cerebral cortex.

"You are bad people. Very bad people. What did your parents teach you?"

They ignore me. I flash to memories of being bullied as a kid. And now they're messing with my kid. The monkey is losing control of the elephant. The caveman is ascendant.

"You're nasty teenagers, and you're going to grow up into nasty adults. And let me tell you, with its history, your country doesn't need any more nasty people."

Did I just play the Nazi card? I did. And I'm not even 100 percent sure they're German. They sounded sort of German. But maybe they're Belgian.

My brother-in-law, Eric, was right. I suffer from the Lake Wobegon Effect. I overestimate my ability to be rational.

But you know what? I need it. I need the Lake Wobegon Effect. I need self-delusion. Otherwise I'd be so depressed about irrationality—and the general apocalyptic state of the world—that I couldn't function.

I have learned this much about myself and my deeply flawed brain: I have to believe, irrationally, against all evidence, that humans can be rational.

CODA

It's been several months since this experiment ended, and I still do a lot of things differently. Tiny things and big things. I shop for air conditioners differently. I watch nature shows differently. I judge human beings differently. Not counting my year of living biblically, the Rationality Project has had the most dramatic, long-lasting effect of all my experiments.

I'm still a highly irrational thinker. But at least I'm aware of it. And sometimes I can stop myself before my thoughts and actions spin out of control.

Here, a small sampling of what's changed:

1. **I make a note every time I'm in a fast-moving grocery line.**

   We all are predisposed to notice and remember the bad stuff. We notice when we're stuck bumper-to-bumper on I-95. Or when we're on a checkout line behind an eighty-two-year-old man paying with a sack of pennies and nickels. Harvard psychologist Daniel Gilbert talks about this in his book *Stumbling on Happiness*. Many of us—me included—have this notion that we always choose the slowest line. But that's only because the frustrating episodes are more emotionally charged and we remember them better. We don't recall all the times we were on a fast-moving, uneventful line. But I try. I say out loud: "Julie, look at that. We chose the airport security line that moved the fastest. We should remember that next time we're on a slow line." I choose to interpret Julie's silence as gratitude.

2. **I spend a few minutes each week reading Michelle Malkin's conservative musings.** I almost typed "conservative rants." But that's just the kind of thing I'm trying to avoid.

   My distant cousin Cass Sunstein—a frighteningly brilliant man who coauthored *Nudge*—tells me that he spends a lot of time reading things that he disagrees with. Even things that annoy him. It's the best buffer against sliding into extremism. He conducted an experiment in Colorado. He gathered a group of moderate liberals from Boulder to discuss politics among themselves for a day. And he got a group of moderate conservatives from Colorado Springs to do the same. The result? The liberals became more liberal, the conservatives more conservative. Diversity was squelched. Extremism flourished. The echo chamber is a dangerous thing.

So I willfully expose myself to the other points of view.

3. I sometimes eat spaghetti for breakfast.

I can't believe just how many of our little daily habits are *not* based on rationality, just custom. Why is some pig meat acceptable in the morning (e.g., bacon, sausages) and other pig meat not (baby-backed ribs and pork chops). No rational reason. If you tried to explain it to Spock, he'd scratch his head. So if I feel like eating pasta for breakfast, I shall eat pasta! Societal norms be damned.

4. I'm more leery of conspiracy theories than ever.

I've never been a fan. I always accepted the idea, for instance, that a maladjusted loser with a bad haircut named Lee Harvey Oswald changed history with nothing more than his bolt-action rifle and some luck. To me, the interesting question is why the human brain finds conspiracies so attractive. I got one answer in a fascinating *Scientific American* article called "Patternicity." Patternicity is the idea that humans are really talented at finding nonexistent patterns in random noise.

Why? Because in caveman times, it was evolutionarily beneficial to find meanings in random noise. The author Michael Shermer explains: If a caveman thought the sound of rustling grass was caused by wind, he was probably right. But what about that 1 in 100 chance he was wrong? My goodness, the price was high. He became lunch for a tiger. So the safe bet was to assume the rustle of the grass was a predator—even if the chances of this being true are minuscule. The result is that our brains are predisposed to paranoia and pattern-seeking. We take all the random JFK assassination data and construct elaborate theories connecting the dots. We look for the tigers where there are none. We find faces in tortillas. We see villains behind grassy knolls.

5. I reserve judgment as long as possible.

First impressions are like South American dictators: overly powerful and unreliable. Thank God my wife, Julie, is compassionate enough to have ignored the first impression's iron grip. As a single woman, Julie had the Three Date Rule. Even if the first date was a catastrophe, Julie had pledged she'd give all guys three dates. My first date with Julie was a catastrophe indeed. (For one thing, I thought I was being progressive and prowoman by suggesting we go Dutch. I've since learned that's not the case. I was being cheap. I've offered to pay her back her twenty-five dollars for eleven years now. She won't take it.) Anyway, thank you, Julie, for withholding judgment. I'm trying to follow your lead.

6. I read menus from the bottom up.

The brain places too much emphasis on the first few options in a list. Restaurateurs know this. But I'm not going to fall for their evil schemes. I'll start at the last entrée and work my way up. (Hmm. It appears I've got a bit of that paranoia I was just talking about.)

7. **I'm filled with hope and despair (not necessarily in that order).**

Despair at how we're all walking around with these defective machines inside our skulls. Hope because we can recognize that fact. And the study of decision making—or behavioral economics, as it's known—offers one possible fix. Yes we can! Behavioral economics seems to be gaining influence daily. As author Dan Ariely points out, the year 2008—which saw the meltdown of the supposedly rational stock market—was a banner year for behavioral economics. Maybe I'm deluded, but I think it will be as powerful as Freudianism was in the 1950s. And hopefully more accurate. In fact, we've got an amateur behavioral economist in the White House now. Obama is a fan of this field. And some of his proposals—such as automatically enrolling people into 401(k)s to take advantage of mental inertia—reflect that.

8. **I'm skeptical of behavioral economics.**

And finally . . . one last thing: You know how I'm convinced that 90 percent of decisions are irrational? That's probably an irrational notion. It's the result of reading book after book about how flawed the brain is. I suffer from the Confirmation Bias. I'm only human.

$$Fame \leq Ego\ (x)^3$$

$$Zen + Focus = Productivity^2$$
$$\sqrt{Brain} \cdot Caveman = \frac{1}{x}$$

$$\frac{Outsourcing^8 + marriage}{12,000\ miles} = 9$$

$$x = \frac{Nudity + Public}{Dignity}$$

$$\sqrt{\frac{Nudity + Public}{Dignity}}$$

$$(Geo.\ Wash. - wig)\ Me = x$$

$$\int_{b}^{a} \frac{husband}{(wife)\ power}$$

$$\frac{Dating + Beauty}{x\ (Cyrano)} \neq Love$$

$$(wife)\ power^3 = x$$

$$\frac{Reason - Emotion}{Behavior} = Insanity$$

$$Truth^n - filter = Chaos$$

Chapter Six

The Truth About Nakedness

It starts out innocently enough. My boss at *Esquire* tells me he's asked the actress Mary-Louise Parker to write an article. This isn't unusual. He often asks notable people to write for the magazine. We recently had Dan Rather write an essay on the importance of using colorful metaphors (a language device that Rather calls "as fun as Saturday night at the Stop 'n' Fight"). So this time, our guest writer is Mary-Louise Parker, who had a role on *The West Wing* at the time.

My boss tells me that I'll be her editor on the essay. The topic? Well, that's not clear yet. It's my job to talk to her and figure it out.

So I e-mail Ms. Parker (mentioning I'm a fan of her work, of course). She suggests she could write an essay about what it's like to be an aunt. That doesn't seem quite right for *Esquire*. She tosses out another couple of topics that sound like they'd put my boss into a stage 3 coma. I start to get worried.

Well, Mary-Louise says, what about this: She could write an essay about what it feels like to pose naked. Now we're talking. I tell my boss—who asks the natural follow-up: will she pose nude for the magazine? The article would need art, after all. I call her back. She agrees.

I have to restrain myself from getting down on my knees and making a burnt offering to this woman. She has just guaranteed my holiday bonus.

I'm about to hang up and tell my boss the good news. But before I can, Mary-Louise has one little—by which I mean deeply disturbing—request.

"I was thinking," she says, "that as the editor of the piece, it would make sense for *you* to appear naked as well."

What now?

"I thought maybe I should choose the photo of you that runs," Mary-Louise continues. "So you can really experience that loss of control and possible objectification."

I can't remember exactly how I reacted to this. But Mary-Louise—in the essay she wrote later—gives a description that sounds pretty accurate. She wrote:

> I was met with some sputtering and somewhat choked, morti-
> fied laughter, the way people laugh when they feel suddenly
> light-headed, or when they view something both compelling
> and grotesque, like, say, two cats having sex, or a child vomit-
> ing into his Easter basket. [A.J.] said he would get back to me.

That rings mostly true. Though for the record, I've never seen a child vomiting into his Easter basket. And if I ever did see one, I don't think I'd laugh. Or at least I'd try to suppress the laugh in case my wife was nearby.

When I get home, I tell Julie about Mary-Louise's idea, and count on her to be equally disturbed. "Oh, you have to do it," she says. "It's only fair." (Julie later confessed that she thought a nude photo in a national magazine would finally force me to start doing ab crunches.) I tell my boss, who is also unnervingly enthusiastic. I mention the possibility of subscription cancellations. "Maybe we could shoot you the way we did Monica Bellucci on our cover," he says. "With caviar on your chest." He's not joking.

I'm relatively new to *Esquire,* and don't have the nerve to say no. So a few days later, I find myself in a cab on the way to the studio with the magazine's design director, who keeps assuring me that there will be nothing edible on my solar plexus and no Mapplethorpian whips in my orifices. This would be very classy, an homage to a famous Yves Saint Laurent nude. *Classy.* An adjective I'm sure Linda Lovelace heard a few times.

In the dim, hangar-sized studio, they pour me chilled sauvignon blanc, put on a Norah Jones CD, hand me a white terrycloth robe, and apologize for not having a fluffer. Everyone has a good laugh at that one.

They still have to adjust the lighting. So I pace back and forth in my robe. In times of stress, I often try to put things in context. Take the long view. In a hundred years, I remind myself, no one will remember this photo. There are six billion people on the planet Earth. No one cares if some midlevel editor at a men's magazine bares his nipples. In ten billion years, the second law of thermodynamics will have run its course, and there won't be humans around to judge, just billions of cold, amoral, lifeless hydrogen atoms bouncing around in the black emptiness.

But every time I try this tactic, another part of my brain plays devil's advocate. You think this will be gone in a hundred years? The Internet has no statute of limitations. This will follow you around forever, like a grand larceny conviction. You think people will be gone? They'll figure out a way to control entropy. They'll figure out a way to keep the database of all embarrassing things you've ever done.

What's that? The crew is ready. Okay. Deep breaths. Ponder the universe in ten billion years. I drop my robe. The air is chilly.

I step in front of the camera. When I'm nervous, I often put my hands in my pockets. This time, I have no pockets. I ease myself onto a round, red cushion (which I hope has been dry-cleaned since the last photo shoot), cross my legs, and try to look dignified.

The photographer is a kind, salt-and-pepper-haired Scotsman named Nigel Parry.

He keeps telling me to relax.

I concentrate really hard on relaxing.

"Try to relax yer face," he says. "You look like yer constipated."

The thing is, it's not really a relaxing situation. In addition to Nigel and his camera, the room has five assistants and a couple of random onlookers. I can't help but notice that all of them are wearing clothes. Whereas I'm not. The balance of power is radically off-kilter.

Nigel snaps a couple of photos.

I try distancing myself. Where would I place this on the spectrum of humiliating episodes in my life? Probably better than the time I inadvertently drooled on the piano during music class in sixth grade and Kim Glickman pointed it out to everyone. But worse than the time I asked Julie's friend when she was due (her baby was six weeks old).

"Okay, now," says Nigel. "Sook in yer goot!"

I stare at him blankly.

"Sook in yer goot!"

My goot? Nigel taps his stomach.

Ah, he's talking about my problematic belly. I sook in some air.

Nigel begins snapping photos. The Frisbee-sized lights flash, making a soft pop, like a snare drum in smooth jazz. I sit. I try to think dignified thoughts. Think of the Romans, the

Greeks. They posed nude and still started civilization as we know it.

I feel vulnerable, yes. There I am, exposed for all to see. But paradoxically, I feel disappointed that no one seems to be looking at me. Nigel has a cadre of cute, young female assistants. They are busy making cell phone calls, chatting about what they heard on NPR that morning, unpacking lenses. My nude form holds about as much allure to them as a wicker chair.

I adjust my pose, lowering my knee. Nigel raises his eyebrows.

"Not like that. I can see your chopper," he says.

I move my knee fast. I don't want my "chopper" on film, even if I know *Esquire* would never publish anything with my chopper exposed.

Esquire is generally opposed to showing the real naughty bits—whether male or female—in their nude photos. This can be quite a creative challenge for the photographers. In my case, Nigel is using a tried-and-true strategy: contortionist, yogalike body positions. Another option would have been props. For our seventieth anniversary, I compiled a list of objects that *Esquire* had used to obscure the nipples on women's breasts over the years: flowers, paperback books, peaches, suspenders, and on and on.

Even though I knew my chopper would be covered, I'd spent the previous three days worrying about its debut in public. I became irrationally obsessed with the idea that it might misbehave. Which is highly unlikely. It's not like I'm thirteen. But what if it does? Stress can do strange things to the body. And if it does, I'd never live it down. I'm terrified of losing control in any situation, and this would seem to be the worst. So I took measures. I've brought along a small black-and-white photo of my late grandmother just in case.

"Your poor grandmother," Julie said, as I scoured photo albums for the picture the last night.

"It's not disrespectful," I said. "It shows my respect for her."

The photo, which I stashed in my shoulder bag, will hopefully never be called into duty.

"Try smiling," says Nigel. "Now serious . . . Now look up for me."

I tilt my chin toward the ceiling.

I've read interviews where celebrities claim to have felt empowered by their nude photo shoot. They learned to embrace the freedom and love their body and throw off the constraining shackles of repressed society. Not me.

I just don't feel comfortable nude. Even when I'm alone in my apartment, I keep my pants zipped. No doubt this comes in part from my ambivalence to my physical self. Maybe it's a Jewish thing—never has a race of people been so disassociated from their bodies. Like many Jews, I spent a lot of my life viewing my body as a way to transport my intellect from place to place. In my twenties, I had a brief half-year fling with weight lifting and StairMaster (guess what? I was single at the time!), but other than that, I haven't logged a lot of hours at Bally Total Fitness. And it shows. My chest has an indentation where you could store a half cup of flour.

I'm much more comfortable exposing the contents of my mind—even when those contents are potentially more humiliating than my chopper. I'll expose my ignorance long before I take off my T-shirt. I'm not sure why I'm okay with laying bare my brain.

Maybe there's a sense of relief in confession. As I discovered while being radically honest, there's freedom in keeping no secrets. Throw all the junk on the lawn and hope the good outweighs the bad.

Perhaps it's so I can beat others to the punch. You're going to make fun of the mole on my nose? I've been doing it for years.

Or maybe it's that when I confess the most embarrassing secrets, there's comfort in knowing that others are just as abnormal as I am. In my book on reading the encyclopedia, I made a throwaway comment about a high school fantasy I had involving pancake batter. A few months later, I got an e-mail from a guy who said he was glad to hear someone shared his passion for pancake batter. It was simultaneously the creepiest letter I've ever gotten, and the most reassuring. Well, more creepy than reassuring, come to think of it.

My sons, incidentally, don't have the same problem with bodily repression. Zane, for instance, loves to get nude. A few months ago, I was on a book tour stop in Cincinnati. I had a prearranged video chat with Julie and Zane. I was on wireless at Starbucks and called them up on my Mac laptop. Julie put the camera on Zane.

And Zane decided, at that moment, that his clothes were restraining, and whipped off his shirt and pants.

I chuckled. Until I started to figure out how this might appear: a thirty-nine-year-old man watching a naked toddler cavort on his computer screen. I glanced around to make sure no one was calling the authorities.

"Okay, then. You can put your clothes back on now."

Julie stayed offscreen. Did she leave? Did she have a pressing appointment?

Zane continued dancing joyfully.

"Julie, can you come back on for a second."

I looked around the Starbucks. I had about forty-five seconds before someone would call *Dateline*.

"Julie? Please."

Nothing.

"Okay, then, daddy has to go now."

I snapped my laptop closed.

Maybe that's the key. It's a generational thing, this privacy gap. My mother still shakes her head in wonder that I use my writing as public therapy. And when I told her that I had to pose naked for my job, she looked at me the way I imagine John Walker Lindh's mom looked at him when he said he was joining the Taliban. Meanwhile, I shake my head in wonder that kids in their twenties "sext" each other during work hours or post MySpace photos of themselves doing naked three-legged races, or whatever the kids are doing nowadays.

Nigel keeps snapping away. I adjust my face. I adjust my butt. I never get comfortable. I try to zone out and think of sandy white beaches. I fail.

"Okay," he says, after half an hour. "We're finished."
Finally.

I grab my clothes, ready for my walk of shame. As I'm leaving, I catch sight of the crew setting up for Mary-Louise. The table fills up with champagne bottles and plates of couscous and grilled chicken. My catering had consisted of a six-pack of Diet Coke and a bottle of wine. An eloquent statement of my place on the celebrity chain. If I thought my dignity was at a low ebb during the photo shoot, the buffet just took the last of it.

CODA

The photos came out a month later. The results were actually much better than they could have been. I swear I almost look buff. Never again will I question the miracle of good lighting. Or of black-and-white film, which makes everything about 50 percent less sleazy. You take a photo of a Delta Nu sorority girl lifting her baby T at Mardi Gras, and if it's in black-and-white, it'll somehow look poignant and profound.

Still, the reaction wasn't good for my ego. You had your expected taunts from coworkers and friends, most saying that I had successfully torpedoed any slim chance I ever had of a real journalistic career. Someone anonymously scribbled on the photo "Time to invest in some Nair"—a reference to my hairy legs. We also got a half-dozen nasty letters. Most complained that my photo, which came right after Mary-Louise Parker's beautiful black-and-white layout, ruined the portfolio. Like enjoying a fantastic tasting menu at a Michelin three-star restaurant, then getting botulism immediately after. "Well, at least there were no subscription cancellations," my boss told me.

I do respect Mary-Louise for putting me through photographic hell. Fame is about exposure, whether it's exposure of your medical records or your past peccadilloes or your on-set tantrums. And she decided to give me a lesson in literal exposure.

And I give her this: She succeeded in her goal. I can never look at a nude picture the same way. I can still admire a nude photo, but I can no longer separate it from the context in which it was created. I can't forget, as Mary-Louise put it, the loss of control and possible objectification.

What were the negotiations like between the editor and the model? Did the person getting photographed feel empowered? And if she felt empowered, was it just a rationalization for allowing herself to be stripped of her pants? What was the dynamic between her and the photographer? What CD was playing to get her in the mood? Did she hate the outcome? Did she like the couscous?

Before this book went to press, I got in touch with Mary-

Louise Parker to ask if she's made any other editors expose themselves. She hasn't. But she did say she was satisfied with the results of our experiment. "I think you learned your lesson," she said. "And I'm supergrateful to your wife. She really pushed you to do it."

I told her that just a month ago, I finally got my first piece of positive feedback on the nude photo. A San Diego man e-mailed me asking for a JPEG of it. (He said he preferred me with my biblical beard, leading me to think he's what you call a "bear." I appeal to a very narrow demographic.) Mary-Louise seemed pleased. "I was actually hoping you'd get a lot of fans in prison to boost your ego. That was my real goal."

$$Fame \leq Ego\,(x)^3$$

$$Zen + Focus = Productivity^2$$

$$\sqrt{Brain \cdot Caveman} = \frac{1}{x}$$

$$\frac{Outsourcing^8 + marriage}{12,000\ miles} = 9$$

$$x = \frac{Nudity + Public}{Dignity}$$

$$\sqrt{\frac{Nudity + Public}{Dignity}}$$

$$(Geo.\ Wash. - Wig)\,Me = x$$

$$\frac{Dating + Beauty}{x\,(Cyrano)} \neq Love$$

$$\int_b^a \frac{husband}{(wife)\,power}$$

$$(wife)\,power^3 = x$$

$$\frac{Reason - Emotion}{Behavior} = Insanity$$

$$Truth^n - filter = Chaos$$

Chapter Seven

What Would George Washington Do?

PREAMBLE

After Julie and I watched the John Adams miniseries on HBO, I had two reactions. The first was unsettling: if I'd been alive in Colonial times, I would *not* have been on the side of the patriots. This is an unpleasant epiphany for someone who's always considered himself moderately patriotic. But I'm convinced of it.

I wouldn't be a king-loving Loyalist, mind you. I'd be somewhere in the middle. John Adams estimated that a third of the country was patriots, a third loyalist, and a third neutral. That'd be me: neutral.

I don't have a revolutionary nature. I'm not confrontational enough. I'd probably grumble about the tax on tea, but in the end, I'd cough up the money rather than putting on a feathered headdress and storming a ship. I mean, I've shelled out $3.45 for a tall pumpkin latte without declaring war on Starbucks. That's truly intolerable.

I knew that the Founding Fathers took a risk. But it didn't sink in quite how breathtaking their leap of faith was. They had to realize that their odds of failure were staggeringly high, like Rob-Schneider-winning-the-Oscar high. And if they did fail, they wouldn't go back to their farms and lick their wounds and play cribbage; they'd all end up swinging from the gallows.

If I'd been alive, I would have sided with Pennsylvania lawyer John Dickinson, who wanted to keep negotiating with Britain, telling the Continental Congress they "should exhaust all peaceful approaches."

"Precisely," I'd say. "If we can get electricity from a kite, we can work out this tax dispute . . ."

So I'm thankful I wasn't born in the eighteenth century.

The second realization was that I wanted to know more about George Washington. In the past, I'd found him the least interesting of the Founding Fathers. Undeniably great, but kind of bland. He was the market leader, sure, but he lacked pizzazz, sort of like Wal-Mart. Give me Ben Franklin and his wry, sometimes randy wisdom. Or Jefferson and his political poetry. Or cantankerous old John Adams, and his strange obsession with his compost pile (see note in back).

But in the miniseries, there was a moment that crystallized Washington's greatness for me in a new way: John Adams had come up with a list of highfalutin titles for the new president ("His Majesty the President" and "His High Mightiness"). Washington scolded him: "Mr. President. That is all."

What restraint! This was a man who could have crowned himself Czar Washington if he'd wanted to. He could have occupied a throne for life. He could have had a harem of big-bustled women. Instead, restraint. This humble act of heroism—which helped assure our democracy didn't become a monarchy—is as impressive to me as Washington's battles. We need more restraint, more civility. I'm writing this as the Dow continues its free fall. And what got us into this? You could argue it was a lack of restraint. Unbridled hunger for power by some rogue emperors of Wall Street.

The next week, while reading Joseph Ellis's biography of George Washington, I stumbled across something extraordinary. Namely, a list Washington wrote called "Rules of Civility and Decent Behaviour in Company and Conversation." It's exactly what it says: an easy-to-read rundown of how to behave while talking, eating, doing business, courting, you name it. There are 110 of them.

Providence—as Washington used to say—has provided me with my next experiment.

First, it's a list of rules. I love those. Frankly, I miss living by the Bible's laws. I miss the stable architecture, the paradoxical freedom from choice. This will be like living biblically, but with a Colonial flavor—less stoning adulterers, more bowing. Second, I'll get a crash course in this remarkable man, the Founding Father in Chief.

And, most important, I'll get to mainline the ideals of a long-ago, seemingly more civil time. I may never become a revolutionary, but maybe I can become a better leader and more dignified human being.

THE LIST

Washington wrote the Rules in his notebook when he was a young man. Rumors to the contrary, he didn't actually come up with the 110 Rules in the first place—they were originally from the pen of a French Jesuit in the late sixteenth century. But he copied them painstakingly by hand. And the list had a deep impact on him. Many historians say it shaped his character throughout his life.

The list itself is an early version of Emily Post mixed with *GQ*, with a dash of Ten Commandments thrown in to give it heft.

The first rule is this:

> Every action done in company ought to be with some sign of
> respect to those that are present.

In other words, be aware of the consequences of your actions on others. An elegant notion that's often ignored in our era of unabashed individualism.

Rule 2 is this:

> When in company, put not your hands to any part of the body
> not usually discovered.

That's right. The second rule that formed the character of our first president? Do not touch your pecker in public.

Turns out this advice is so important, and the habit so rampant among eighteenth-century men, it merits repeating just a few rules later.

> Rule 11: Shift not yourself in the sight of others.

Okay? No pocket pool, as we called it in eighth grade. And ladies, no adjusting the bra straps.

This much is clear: the list has quite a range.

Some rules are general, some wildly specific. Some reflect the era, some could have been written this morning. And they will affect every part of my existence:

- The way I talk ("mock not at anything important," "speak
  not of doleful things in a time of mirth or at the table")

- The way I think ("in all causes of passion, let reason govern")
- The way I laugh (not "too much at any public spectacle")
- The way I squash bugs ("kill no vermin, or fleas, lice, ticks, etc., in the sight of others")
- The way I sit ("keep your feet firm and even")
- The way I eat (don't complain about the food, don't "gaze about while you are drinking")
- The way I treat my friends ("Show nothing to your friend that may affright him")
- The way I treat my bosses ("In company of those of higher quality than yourself, speak not 'til you are asked a question")

Oh, and by the way, I will not be spitting for the next few weeks. Washington's Rules were very opposed to spitting. And if I see spittle on the ground, I should "dexterously cover it up" with my foot. (For the full list of 110 Rules, see Appendix A.)

BASIC TRAINING

Before I try to spend a few weeks behaving like George Washington, I figure I'll consult a man whose full-time job is to behave like Washington. His name is Dean Malissa. He's the Sean Penn of George Washington impersonators. Or interpreters, I found out later. That's the preferred term.

Malissa agrees to meet me and invites me to see him in action at Valley Forge, Pennsylvania. So on a late September day, I join a group tour at Valley Forge. I'm standing next to Phineas Folger, a Quaker merchant who is wearing a Huskies baseball cap and is getting sunscreen applied to his face by his mom.

We've all been assigned a Colonial character to portray—

it's part of the tour's living-history shtick. I'm Charles Carter, a "gentleman of the highest honor."

On my other side is a seamstress named Abigail (aka Irene, a nurse from Seattle). She looks like a naturally aged Diane Keaton—and she's a Washington groupie. She spends her vacations visiting places where Washington has slept. I tell her about my project on the rules of civility.

"That's what I love about George Washington," she says. "He embodies those rules. He was virtuous. He did things for the right reasons—out of service."

She pauses.

"Not like that Jefferson. He liked to stir things up. He'd do something awful, then say 'it wasn't me!' "

Irene throws up her hands in mock "What? I'm innocent!" pose.

We stop for a Colonial-themed dinner (the dessert includes Martha Washington's coconut balls, which caused some snickering among the teenage congressional delegates). And then we walk to Washington's headquarters. The door swings open and out strides George dressed in smart yellow pants and a blue waistcoat. It's kind of startling how much Dean looks like our first president. He breaks six feet, has the president's substantial nose, and a mane of white hair tied behind his head. (Later, I'll learn that his Achilles heel is eye color—Washington had blue, Dean has brown. For close-up film work, Dean puts in blue contact lenses.)

"What I am about to share is of the utmost sensitivity and I need to be certain that all of you will keep this confidence," says Dean-as-Washington.

He tells us that his spies inform him that the British plan to evacuate Philadelphia imminently. They've ordered all their laundry to be returned immediately.

"My friends, we entreat your fervent prayers."

And now, he'll take questions.

On the back of our name badges, the Valley Forge folks have suggested questions for our characters to ask General Washington.

The delegate from New York asks the old chestnut: "Are your teeth made out of wood?"

"No, they are not," replies Washington. "I have problems with my teeth because my father had very bad teeth. I also like to crack Brazil nuts with my teeth and that's not a very smart thing to do. I do have false teeth and they are made of animal bone."

This I knew from my days reading the encyclopedia: they're actually a mixture of human teeth and ivory from elephants and hippos.

"General," I call out. I figure I should get in the spirit and read the question on my name badge. "I mean no disrespect, General, but I have heard rumors you married for money. Is that true?"

Washington looks at me sternly.

"That is inappropriate, sir."

"Sorry. I'm just reading what's on the card."

"The truth is that Mrs. Washington was an exceptionally wealthy widow . . . But sir, it was something very magical that transpired between us and I will leave it at that."

Dean's right. The Valley Forge folks set me up. The question is a very uncivil invasion of privacy. In fact, I've been thinking that just researching the life of Washington is an un-Washingtonian invasion of his privacy. Rule 18 warns us, for instance, not to read other people's letters.

The problem is, much of what we know about George Washington is based on his private letters, released to the public after his death. How would Washington feel about this? You think he'd be happy that we all know he apparently had a crush on Sally Fairfax, his married neighbor? He wrote her a letter saying, "The World has no business to know the object of my Love, declared in this manner to you when I want to conceal it."

And what about the receipt for cantharides that was found among his letters? The other name for cantharides is Spanish fly. Biographer Paul Johnson argues that Washington might have needed the Spanish fly as a very primitive form of Viagra. (If Johnson is right, which I'm not sure he is, then the Washington Monument is the single most ironic tribute on planet Earth.)

With Washington, the dilemma we face is between a respect for his privacy and the importance of understanding history. And it seems history generally trumps privacy. Thank God I'm not going to be a great man. Poor Obama. In a hundred years, historians will be combing through his Google searches and pharmacy receipts.

By the way, Washington probably did marry partly for money.

The next morning, I meet Dean at his home, which sits on the border of a woody park in suburban Philadelphia. He greets me at the door wearing white shorts and a mustard-colored "Don't Tread on Me" T-shirt, his long white hair freed from its ponytail.

"I hate the long hair," he tells me. "But it's all about accuracy. Men in Washington's day wore wigs but Washington never did. He would powder his hair for formal events, but he would consider himself a soldier and a farmer. He did not wear a wig."

We enter the house, and I'm met with an explosion of George Washington memorabilia. George Washington paintings on the wall. George Washington books on the shelves. George Washington waistcoats and breeches in the closet. George Washington booze in the kitchen—Madeira was his drink of choice.

We sit down, and Dean tells me about life as Washington's doppelganger. He's quite busy, working at both Valley Forge and Mount Vernon, the latter gig coming to him after another Washington interpreter retired.

"They were actually considering a nationwide search," Dean says.

"Really?" I say. "That could have been a good reality show. *America's Next George Washington.*"

"I hate reality television," he says. "I actually have great distaste for most television. Portraying Washington has sensitized me with regard to the devolution of our world and our country. The lack of courtesy, the lack of civility, the lack of a self-starting populace. The whole idea of virtue and honor is becoming more and more difficult to find. So your comment about reality television strikes a nerve because it is the pus at the top of the pimple. It is everything that I hate."

"Yeah," I lie. "I don't watch it much, either."

I think I just got schooled. Hoping to redeem myself, I shift gears quickly. I ask him if he thinks I can learn from the 110 Rules.

"Yes. Just remember Washington's personal credo: Deeds, not words. He may not have been the greatest thinker of his day, but he took the greatest ideas of his day and translated them into action.

"He tended to be very reticent and take in a lot without responding," says Dean. "I cannot portray him that way. Or else I'd lose my audience."

So was our first president really different from us? Was he really more civil and decent? Yes, says Dean. Just look at politicians today. "If George Washington knew that politicians in

America *run* for the presidency, he would be appalled. A gentleman does not run for president. He *stands* for the presidency.
Running might make him less able to govern for the good of the
people, and dispense justice."

He also would have kept us from this economic mess we're
descending into. "In Washington's Farewell Address, he warns
us against mortgaging the future of our children and grandchil-
dren. And that's exactly what we've done."

Dean's so passionate about Washington, I feel guilty that I
overlooked G.W. all these years. He says he thinks of Washington as the American Moses—the right man at the right time.
And, like the seamstress/nurse from Seattle, Dean very civilly,
very politely disses Jefferson: "The more one reads about Jefferson, the more one becomes aware of the great difference between his actions and his words."

As I leave, we bump into Dean's wife, Debbie, who works in
Jewish education in Philly. I ask her how she likes being married
to George Washington. She hates the hair, but overall it's a
pretty fun life.

"Just don't call her Martha or she'll sock you in the jaw,"
Dean says.

"What's wrong with Martha?"

"She was old and chubby and was about this high," says
Debbie.

I promise not to call her Martha.

"Remember," Dean says, as he bids me good-bye. "Deeds.
Not words."

WALK LIKE GEORGE WASHINGTON

My meeting with Dean made me realize one huge secret to
Washington's success: his appearance. He just looked dignified.

He strode the earth like a great man. Even before our CNN-saturated era, appearances counted.

Washington had a born advantage in the dignity department: he was tall, about six foot two, which was gargantuan back then. A cranky John Adams (who was five feet seven) once whined that Washington's height won him the presidency. Adams grumbled that, like King Saul, Washington was "chosen because he was taller by the head than the other Jews."

But Washington carried that towering frame with aplomb. "There is not a monarch in Europe who would not look like a *valet de chambre* by his side," said Benjamin Rush, a Founding Father and doctor.

I've decided deportment is an appropriate place to start the Washington Project. I'll begin with the exterior and move on to the mind. It's in the spirit of the Rules. An impressive 47 of the 110 Rules focus on exteriors: how to walk, how to sit, how to smile.

Namely:

No fidgeting or bouncing of the legs
No shaking the head
Sit with your feet firmly planted on the floor, not crossed

And the face! The gentleman in Colonial times wore a Botox-like visage.

Rule 12: "Roll not the eyes; lift not one eyebrow higher than the other, wry not the mouth."

It's the first day of my experiment, and I'm doing my best to walk around New York like George Washington. It's not easy. I feel like my body is a colt, and I'm a cowboy trying to break it.

I'm standing up straight. More than straight. Dean instructed me on the proper posture in Washington's day: chest thrust out, shoulders back, very Dudley Do-Right.

In my regular life, I amble around looking like Hominid No. 3 in those evolution charts. Partly, it's out of laziness. But partly, it feels odd to me to thrust out my chest, almost presumptuous. During my biblical year, I learned that the Talmud suggests that we *not* walk in a jaunty, upright manner. Be humble in your posture, it says. Stooped shoulders were a sign of respect.

No more of that. I shall stand tall. And it's strange—a rigid posture does make me feel more decisive, more confident. I feel like issuing some executive orders.

"I'll have four C batteries, please," I intone to the pharmacy guy, my delivery crisp.

"Yes, sir."

Has he ever called me "sir"? I don't think so.

I keep my face still. Washington was the original stone face. Some historians say Washington's elaborate dentures—a contraption involving metal springs—were so uncomfortable, they forced his mouth into the dour position you see on the front of the dollar bill. But he was also just following the Rules.

"The idea of these etiquette laws were to set themselves apart from the common people," says C. Dallett Hemphill, author of a history of American manners, *Bowing to Necessities*, whom I'd called to get some perspective. "You wanted to have self-mastery, so you could demonstrate to the uncouth that you had self-control. And controlling the body and face was part of this self-mastery. Washington was famous for his self-mastery."

Julie didn't notice my new controlled face—at least not consciously—until the weekend. It was my niece's bat mitzvah. There was a photo booth. Julie asked me to join her, so I went in with her and she pulled the curtain. The camera flashed four times.

The photos came back with her sticking out her tongue à la Gene Simmons and crossing her eyes, while I stared ahead serenely, not smiling, not frowning, like a department store mannequin.

She looked at me, disbelieving.

"I am trying not to loll the tongue or wry the mouth," I said.

At which she violated Rule 12 and rolled her eyes.

STAY ALOOF LIKE GEORGE WASHINGTON

It's been a week. I'm being as civil as I can—lots of pleases and thank-yous, standing up when people return to the table, no spitting in the sink when I wash my hands. But I'm already having second thoughts about this experiment.

I want to be more civil, yes. But do I want to be like George Washington? Here are the adjectives his biographers use: *aloof, reserved,* even *arctic.*

He'd happily sit in silence at the dinner table. He didn't often toss back ale with his soldiers because he thought it'd erode his dignity. After the meal, he'd sometimes read the newspaper aloud to guests, which doesn't sound like a fun Friday night. And let me tell you, if you hung out with him, you weren't going to be spewing a lot of milk through your nose. The man wasn't much for jokes. (George Washington's biographers always point out a couple of gags he made during his life, just to show he's human. My favorite is in a letter he wrote to a just-married friend. Washington advised him to "make the first onset upon his fair Del Toboso with vigor, that the impression may be deep, if it cannot be lasting or frequently renewed." That's the closest G.W. got to working blue.)

I like the idea of being civil. But does it require me to be an ice king? How closely aligned are dignity and keeping your dis-

tance? Because, as the professor points out, yes, the idea of etiquette is partly about respect—but it's also partly about elitism.
No sir, I'm not like those rubes. I've got me some manners.

DRINK LIKE GEORGE WASHINGTON

Luckily, there are enough inspiring tales in my Washington bi-
ographies to keep me going. Yesterday, a week into the project,
I read about one of my favorite examples of his civility:

After the British surrendered at Yorktown, the general told
his men, "Do not cheer. History will huzzah for us." I'm not sure
how his troops felt about this—"Um, we'd really like to huzzah
now"—but it's a beautiful and noble thought.

And it's straight out of the Rules: "Show not yourself glad at
the misfortune of another though he were your enemy."

I try it out tonight. Julie and I go out to dinner with our
friends Paul and Lisa. The drinks arrive.

"Here's to the self-destruction of the Republican Party,"
says Paul, lifting his beer.

We're in the middle of the Obama/McCain presidential race,
and the Republicans do seem to be intent on immolating themselves.

Lisa raises her glass. Julie raises hers. I refuse.

"You're a Republican now?"

"No, I just don't think it's civil to gloat."

Paul lets out a noise somewhere between a laugh and a
groan.

"You know, I think he's got a point," says Julie. She puts her
glass down. Yes! Support from Julie during one of my experiments—that's heaven.

"Fine. What would you like to toast to?"

"Freedom from mobs as well as kings." A traditional Founding Fathers toast.

It's interesting. The Rules don't forbid you from feeling gleeful at your enemy's demise. The rule is, Don't *show* that you're gleeful. It's almost the opposite of Radical Honesty. Put an extreme filter between your brain and your mouth.

The Rules are like cognitive therapy—behave civilly, and eventually you'll think civilly. The Rules are a rejection of what Richard Brookhiser, in his excellent intro to a 1997 reprinting of the 110 Rules, calls the "cult of authenticity." Why should we show all our emotions? Why should we always try to be true to our natural selves? What if our natural selves are assholes? Stalin was true to himself.

In times like these, I love Washington's repression. Or, as he might say, self-mastery.

GREET LIKE GEORGE WASHINGTON

George Washington hated shaking hands—another mark in his favor. At receptions, he'd stand with one hand on his sword and one hand holding a tricorner hat, leaving zero hands available for shaking. And Dean Malissa told me the hat wasn't even a real hat. It was specially made with a hole in it to hide his hand.

As a mild OCD sufferer, I support Washington completely. His handshake-phobia, however, came a few decades before the germ theory. It was all part of his aloofness and dislike of physical contact. Washington preferred the old-school greeting: bowing, in accordance with Rule 26: "Make a reverence, bowing more or less according to the custom of the better bred."

So I've decided to follow suit. When I visited him, Dean gave me a tutorial:

"When you bow, you must sit back on your rear leg. Oh, and we have no monarchy in this country, so you keep your eyes straight. You look into the eyes.

"If you're bowing formally, you put your best foot forward and you turn out your toes to present your calf. If you're bowing to a man, your calf projects your power. If you're bowing to a woman, your calf projects something else."

Something else? What something else? Was there a saying, the bigger the calf, the bigger the . . .

Dean smiles mysteriously. (He later told me that's exactly what he meant. Legend has it there were even prosthetic wooden calves you could stuff in your socks to appear more manly.)

For the last week, I've avoided handshakes altogether in favor of the bow. There's been a clear split in reactions.

There are the reciprocators. I met this lawyer at a cocktail party my wife took me to.

"This is Alex, he's a friend of Barbara's."

Alex stuck out his hand.

I did a quick, shallow bow. He looked startled. And then he did an even deeper bow.

I took that as a challenge and executed the full Dean Malissa lean-back-and-present-your-calf-and-bend-90-degrees-at-the-waist bow.

He responded with a graceful arm swoop and a doffing of his baseball cap.

On the other hand, there are the insulted. Yesterday, I met my friend David for lunch, and he brought his business associate Terry, whom I'd never met. Terry stuck out his hand. I ignored it, and bowed to him, presenting my calf. He looked startled.

He kept holding out his hand. He would not take it down.

I bowed again, this time more quickly.

And yet that hand—it stayed out there.

I bowed a short cursory bow, just a little head dip.

"You want me to say something in Japanese?"

"I'm trying not to shake hands."

"It's all right. You can shake hands."

"No, I'm trying not to."

"Come on."

We stood there for ten seconds, playing chicken with the salutations. Finally, he took down his hand, but the lunch was halting and awkward.

Historically, the handshake was seen as a democratic gesture. William Penn was a big proponent, and scandalized some upper-crust types by shaking hands with Indians. But nowadays, I think the bow has more benefits. Though it may seem pretentious, it's actually deeply humbling. Just lowering yourself before someone—the universal symbol of modesty—makes you feel more respectful. Behavior shapes your thoughts.

REFRAIN FROM ANGER LIKE GEORGE WASHINGTON

George Washington is known for controlling his emotions. What's remarkable about this is what a struggle it must have been for him. He wasn't born with a Zen attitude. Just the opposite. Below his placid exterior, he was a burbling witch's cauldron of emotions.

And when he did lose control—which was more often than he liked—oh man it was ugly. "Few sounds on earth could compare with that of General Washington swearing a blue streak," wrote his private secretary.

Gilbert Stuart—the artist who painted the portrait on the

dollar bill—said he saw in Washington's face "the strongest and most ungovernable passions, and had he been born in the forests, it was [my] opinion that he would have been the fiercest man among the savage tribes."

But as the Rules say, "Use no reproachful language against anyone, neither curse nor revile," and "In all causes of passion, permit reason to govern."

I worked on restraining my wrath during my Bible year, but it's a struggle that's never over. Today I get my chance to practice Washington-style anger management. Here's what happened: since I have no office, and since I have three extremely loud boys, my mother-in-law lends me her studio apartment when she's away on a trip. I go there during the days to write.

Last week, she came back a day early, before I'd had a chance to clean up the empty soda cans and dishes.

She was not happy. I called to apologize, which was the Washingtonian thing to do: he could be great at saying sorry.

"Hello, Barbara. It's your son-in-law calling to apologize."

"This is not working out," she says. "We have different standards of cleanliness. You're going to have to find somewhere else to work."

"Well, I know I made a mistake, but—"

Damn. My cell phone cut out. I dial her back. She answers.

"Hi, Barbara. Sorry about that, my cell phone seems to have died."

"No, it didn't. I hung up."

"You hung up on me?"

"I said what I wanted to say, and then I hung up."

"Wow."

Now, normally, my reaction would have been mild annoyance mixed with amusement. She's a character, my mother-in-law. The first words I ever heard her utter were "I need a drink."

(She'd had a bad parking experience.) So generally I'm able to enjoy her quirks.

But I'm hyperaware of manners right now. And to get hung up on? That was rude. *Highly* uncivil. I've been treated better by parking cops.

I start to sweat. I punch in her number, ready to reproach her and curse and revile. Wait. I can't do that. Follow George Washington's lead. I click off.

That afternoon, I sit down to write a letter to Barbara. I love the Colonial style of writing—the roundabout phraseology. "It is not without reluctance that I bring this up," I start. "But I wanted to endeavor to elucidate my concern."

The beauty part is, this formal, repressed language actually makes me less angry. How can I be foaming at the mouth when I use words like *elucidate*?

I sign it "A. J. Jacobs."

Julie laughs at me. "You probably don't need the last name."

At least I didn't write "Your humble and obedient servant," the way Dean signs his e-mails.

I drop the note off at Barbara's apartment building. The next day, Barbara comes over to talk.

"I'm sorry if I offended you," she says.

"And I am sorry about the cleanup."

"I just thought it was better to get off the phone quickly so nothing escalated."

"You liked the letter?"

"It was very formal."

"Thank you."

It's possible you could call the letter passive-aggressive. But the Rules encourage passive aggression. And I have to say, passive aggression gets a bad rap nowadays. It may not be appropriate in all occasions, but it's a lot better than aggressive aggression.

IGNORE GOSSIP LIKE GEORGE WASHINGTON

Remember how Dean said George Washington has sensitized him to just how uncivil these times are? I think about that a lot.

These *are* some seriously uncivil times. It's been two weeks, and I made the mistake of looking at some comments about myself on the Internet. It's a terrible habit, and I've been trying to kick it for years. But I keep sneaking back on.

Today, I clicked on a YouTube video of me speaking about my Bible book. Among the comments:

"His voice is sooo annoying." (I'm a tad nasal, sort of Truman Capote without the drawl. Or maybe late-model Arnold Horshack.)

"Does he remind anyone else of Beaker from the Muppets?"

Another called me a "rabbit man" (a reference to my slightly buck teeth, I think, or maybe my love of lettuce).

I read the comments with my finger on the QUIT button, so that if I get to a particularly harsh one, I can zap the window off my screen.

These are brutal times. But the question is, Are they any more brutal than Washington's era? I'm not so sure. There was some scurrilous, nasty stuff going on. Consider James Callender, a sleazeball journalist would have done quite well as an Internet troll. Thomas Jefferson hired Callender to write nasty articles about John Adams. When Callendar felt he didn't get paid properly by Jefferson, he turned on Jefferson, writing a scathing article about Jefferson's private life. He was the first to expose Jefferson's affair with Sally Hemings.

Luckily for me, of all the Founding Fathers, George Washington does seem the most civil. He wasn't much of a gossip. And he didn't believe others' gossip, to the point of naïveté. In

Washington's second term, Thomas Jefferson started spreading nasty rumors about Washington—including that he was senile. Washington was told, but refused to believe Jefferson would say such things. Washington looked for the best in people. He was no Machiavellian.

It makes me like George Washington a lot more. And Jefferson? Maybe I'm just falling for the pro-Washington propaganda, but he does seem seriously flawed.

WEEP LIKE GEORGE WASHINGTON

It's late October, just a couple weeks until the election. As a moderate New York liberal, I'm legally required to vote for Obama. But I have to say, I'm looking forward to my two minutes behind the curtain, unlike voting for John Kerry four years ago, which felt like wiping the inside of the microwave oven—something I needed to do, but I knew wasn't going to be much fun.

Everyone compares Obama to his fellow Illinois man Abe Lincoln. But since I'm doing this project, I see everything through Washington-colored lenses.

And to me, Obama is the political offspring of our first president. Consider:

- Obama (aka No-Drama Obama) is famous for his mastery over his emotions. In true Washingtonian style, Obama even controls his facial muscles.
- He's deliberative. Like our first president, he doesn't lead from his gut. Thomas Jefferson wrote that "perhaps the strongest feature in [Washington's] character was prudence, never acting until every circumstance, every consideration was maturely weighed." Obama got slammed

as indecisive for not voting on a bunch of U.S. Senate bills. But I have a soft spot for reasoned indecision.

- He says he plans to surround himself with a cacophony of voices. Before Lincoln's team of rivals, there was Washington's team of rivals. I'm surprised the agrarian idealist Jefferson and the industrial realist Hamilton didn't claw each other's eyes out.

- He styles himself a postpartisan president. Washington was prepartisan. He was appalled when the country split into political parties.

I know. I've been swept away by this Obama thing. I've lost all perspective. I feel like the poet in the 1789 *New Hampshire Recorder* who wrote:

Behold the matchless Washington—
His glory has eclips'd the sun;
The luster of his rays so bright
'Tis always day, there's no more night.

The next day, I call Dean to give him an update. I tell him that I had been skeptical of George Washington early on, but now I'm liking him more and more.

"I remember I was reading *Washington's Secret War* by Thomas Fleming," he tells me. "I was on vacation at Villa del Sol in Mexico—that's the beach in *Shawshank Redemption,* by the way. It's where they always dreamed of going. I must have had a couple of Coronas. I put the book down in my lap. And I started to cry.

"And my wife says, 'What's wrong?'

"And I said, 'It's not what's wrong. It's what's right.'

"This man is amazing."

I'm glad Dean feels comfortable enough to tell me about his crying jags. Maybe it's because his hero was also a weeper. I wouldn't have thought it, seeing as he's so famously stoic. But Washington wept in public several times. At the end of the Revolutionary War, Washington gave a speech to his men about how proud he was of them, and had tears streaming down his face.

A few days later, at 11 P.M., Julie and I are watching TV in bed. John McCain has just given a highly civil and decent concession speech.

Barack Obama strides onstage in Chicago's Grant Park.

"If there is anyone out there who still doubts that America is a place where all things are possible; who still wonders if the dream of our founders is alive in our time; who still questions the power of our democracy, tonight is your answer," he tells the nation.

Julie is crying. Jesse Jackson is crying. I'm having trouble controlling my face muscles as well.

This is an amazing moment. Even if Obama did *run* for president instead of *stand* for president, it's still an amazing moment. I hope Obama turns out to be a Washingtonian leader in the original sense and not Washingtonian in the Beltway sense. We'll see.

EVOLVE LIKE GEORGE WASHINGTON

As my project wraps up, I've got a hankering to see George Washington in action again. Dean isn't performing this weekend. But another reenactor is slated to appear at a French and Indian War battle near Pittsburgh. It's where George Washington first tasted the military life, fighting on the side of his future enemies, the British.

I get to the field right in time for battle. French forces, about a hundred of them, dressed in white uniforms with tall black hats, advance slowly from the left side of the field. The British forces advance even more slowly. It's an organized and polite battle—the two sides take turns shooting at each other, never letting the affair descend into unpleasant chaos. The muskets—which are loaded with gunpowder but no bullets—sound like very loud microwave popcorn. Pop, pop, pop! The guns blow smoke rings that float up and disappear in the trees.

Here in the spectator section, I'm standing among the members of the Boy Scout troop from Allegheny County.

"Two AK-47s is all they need," says one Boy Scout. "Mow those Frenchies right down."

The Brits have a kilt-wearing bagpipe player who walks behind the soldiers blowing a mournful tune. War was still brutal back then, but at least it came with a lovely soundtrack.

The soldiers on both sides start dropping to the ground. Every few seconds, another one slumps and splays on the field. They are good splayers, these soldiers, arms and legs bent in all sorts of acute and obtuse angles.

The Brits are almost wiped out. The head British officer surrenders to the French, who take him away for a vigorous pedicure, or whatever they did to their fellow gentlemen/officers.

It's been forty-five minutes and so far, no George Washington in sight. I ask the Boy Scout leader where the colonel is.

He tells me Washington wasn't in this particular battle, but is around somewhere.

"You know where he's camped?"

"He might know," says the Scout leader.

He points to a stout reenactor in a green jacket and a brown felt hat. He's a Pennsylvania infantryman.

"Excuse me!" I call out. "I'm looking for George Washington."

The Pennsylvania soldier stomps over to me.

"Colonel George Washington? You're looking for Colonel Washington?"

"Yes."

"The brash, arrogant young man?" He shakes his head. "He got us into this war. Brash and arrogant he is."

I laugh. I haven't heard such blatant anti-Washington rhetoric. It seems almost sacrilegious. I've had my issues with George Washington, but this soldier seems unduly harsh.

The soldier, I find out, is Mike, a veteran reenactor.

"Did you fight in the battle today?" I ask.

"No, I hurt my knee and figured the mud is slippery, so maybe I should sit this one out."

Mike's been doing French and Indian and Revolutionary War reenactments for forty years, a survivor of about eight hundred events. He buys gunpowder in bulk, he tells me.

"So that's real gunpowder?"

He nods.

"You ever use live ammunition?"

"No," he says. Most reenactors are exceedingly careful with their guns—you're not even supposed to jam the gunpowder down with a ramrod.

"Someone might forget about it and leave the ramrod in there," explains Mike. "And then it'll fly downfield and spear a soldier on the other side. It happens."

He pauses. "Especially with Civil War reenactors. Those guys have no idea what they're doing. Horrible. Horrible."

I wasn't aware of this—the cold war between the Civil War and Revolutionary War reenactors. But Mike assures me the Civil War troops are a problem.

"We've had converts," Mike tells me.

I return to the subject of Colonel George Washington.

"I'm not a fan of the young Washington," Mike says. "He turned out to be a good man when he was older. But as a young man? He was subversive. He tried to undermine his superiors. Watch what you read about him, because he's glorified."

Mike didn't know where the brash colonel was, so I wandered off. Finally, the wife of a French soldier pointed out the young officer a few hundred yards down the path. He had the red hair of a young George Washington, and a blue long coat. I approached.

"Colonel Washington?" I said.

"Yessir."

"I'm from a gazette in New York called *Esquire*."

"Oh," he says. "How can I help you?"

"I talked to a man just now who called you brash and arrogant."

Washington laughs.

"That's got to be Mike," he says.

"Yes, that's who it was."

He scoffs. "He's just jealous he has to wear that ugly green uniform."

The young George Washington—who, when not commanding troops, spends his time as a geologist named Bryan Cunning—is jovial and chatty. He doesn't have Dean's gravitas, and certainly breaks character more often than Dean. I thank him for his time. He tries to shake my hand, but I bow instead.

"Oh yes," he says. "Right."

As I drive back to New York, I think more about Mike's unexpected rant than about Bryan's Washington interpretation. Many of my books talk about how Washington evolved for the better as he got older. But no one had put it as succinctly as Mike. Washington was a selfish twit who turned into one of the greatest men of his time.

The authors James MacGregor Burns and Susan Dunn come close in their book *George Washington*.

In 1772, they write, Washington was a "military leader who had met with more failure than success. An acquisitive planter, a harsh slave owner. A politician more interested in local roads and hogs than international affairs. An ambitious, self-made man hungry for notice. A class-conscious member of gentry who enjoyed dancing, cards and fox hunting. . . . Could this elitist southerner with aristocratic inclinations fathom and embody the hopes of revolutionary Americans and reformers around the world?"

In a word: yes.

By the end of his life, as Joseph Ellis says, Washington was defined not by his selfishness but by his sacrifices. He sacrificed his cushy life on the farm to take the presidency. And after eight years, he sacrificed the chance for absolute power by walking away from it (a move that Britain's King George III said made him the greatest man on earth).

In my more cynical moments, I think that people can't really change. In these moments I think: once a jerk, always a jerk. But Washington proves me wrong. He went from being self-centered to, if not a saint, then certainly a mensch. Maybe there's hope for us all.

CODA

The biggest impact of this experiment was to drive home the point: be wary of first impressions. And second impressions. And third. I learned this in my Rationality Project, but no one shows it better than Washington.

The more I read about him, the more fascinating he became. So complex, so full of contradictions, so continuously evolving.

He seems torn between his two sides. The aristocratic side of him was highly aware of class distinctions. (Earlier in his life, he complained about the poorer farmers, whom he called "barbarians.") And yet, the democratic side rejected the title of king and treated commoners with respect. He was distant, but friendly. He was full of rage but rarely expressed it. And he was inspiring. He was so inspiring, there's a chance that, if I'd been around in the eighteenth century and had drunk enough Madeira, I'd actually have joined the patriots to follow him.

Did this project change my life forever? Certainly not like the experiments in living by the Bible or attempting total rationality. Washington's Rules had a lesser impact. They never sunk into my bones.

That said, I do think about this experiment often. I like Richard Brookhiser's point that our society overvalues "authenticity," the notion that we have to be true to ourselves. *"Well, that's just human nature,"* we say when excusing some atrocious action.

If Washington had been true to himself—or at least his baser instincts—he'd have been an angry brat all his life. The results would have been disastrous. We'd all be eating bangers and mash, and July 4th would be just another day without fireworks or Will Smith movies.

Whenever I'm true to my basest instincts, I'm a schadenfreude-loving, rumor-mongering, selfish son of a bitch. That's the easy road. The hard part is trying to stand up straight, refrain from injurious words, refuse to be glad at the misfortune of others, remain skeptical of flying rumors, and, of course, shift not your private parts.

$$\text{Fame} \le \text{Ego}(x)^3$$

$$\text{Zen} + \text{Focus} = \text{Productivity}^2$$

$$\sqrt{\text{Brain}} \cdot \text{Caveman} = \frac{1}{x}$$

$$\frac{\text{Outsourcing}^8 + \text{marriage}}{12,000 \text{ miles}} = 9$$

$$x = \frac{\text{Nudity} + \text{Public}}{\text{Dignity}}$$

$$\sqrt{\frac{\text{Nudity} + \text{Public}}{\text{Dignity}}}$$

$$(\text{Geo. Wash.} - \text{wig})\,\text{Me} = x$$

$$\frac{\text{Dating} + \text{Beauty}}{x(\text{Cyrano})} \ne \text{Love}$$

$$\int_b^a \frac{\text{husband}}{(\text{wife})\text{power}}$$

$$(\text{wife})\text{power}^3 = x$$

$$\frac{\text{Reason} - \text{Emotion}}{\text{Behavior}} = \text{Insanity}$$

$$\text{Truth}^n - \text{filter} = \text{Chaos}$$

PHOTO ILLUSTRATION BY F. SCOTT SCHAFER

Chapter Eight

My Life as a Beautiful Woman

I've been a beautiful woman for fifty days, and no one has compared me to a summer's day. No one has said my lips are like rose blossoms or my throat is as smooth as alabaster.

Men don't have time for that anymore. We live in the age of transparency. Say what you mean and mean what you say. As in:

"You are a very pretty lady."

"I think you are very attractive."

"You look hot."

I've been approached by more than six hundred men, and that's one of the big themes I've discovered in their method: cut to the chase.

The directness has its charms, but like everything else about being a beautiful woman, it has its dark side as well. One suitor tried to seduce me with this line: "I would like to stalk you." Another said, "I am in a committed relationship but am looking for a girl on the side." Are these guys honest? Sure. To the point? Yes. Creepy? As hell.

I'm getting ahead of myself. Let me back up. I stumbled into this experiment as a hot woman. This one wasn't premeditated. As a general rule, I dislike female impersonation. I have too many bad associations of men in skirts—Benny Hill, Uncle

Miltie, Idi Amin. But sometimes there are good—or at least excusable—reasons to pose as a female.

The reason in this case is my two-year-old son's nanny, Michelle. She's a stunning woman. Before my wife and I hired her, I thought that hot nannies existed only in vintage *Penthouse* Forum letters and Aaron Spelling dramas. But Michelle—though I've changed her name for this book—is real. She's twenty-seven and looks like a normal-lipped Angelina Jolie. She's sweet, funny, has a smile straight out of a cruise-line commercial, and wears adorable tank tops.

No one can believe quite how beautiful my nanny is. Among our friends, my wife's sanity is questioned about twice a week. Michelle is so enchanting, my wife has actually given me permission to have an affair with her, à la *Curb Your Enthusiasm*. Of course, she made the offer only because she knew there was no chance Michelle would ever be interested. Michelle is too sweet, too Catholic, too loyal, too young. It's like giving me permission to become a linebacker for the Dolphins.

In any case, Michelle remains bafflingly single. So my wife and I decided to help her find a boyfriend. How about Internet dating? we suggested. Michelle balked. She's shy. She's not a big fan of e-mail. Her Internet's down. And aren't all the guys on those sites the kind that have a drawerful of ball gags?

We told her that's an outdated stereotype. We'd help her out. Or I would, since my job is editing and writing. I'd sign her up for a dating site, create a profile, sift through her suitors, and cowrite her e-mails. I'd be her online bouncer, bodyguard, censor, and Cyrano. All she'd have to do is give me some input and allow a few guys to buy her lattes.

She agreed. And even started to like the idea. She wrote her own introductory essay. ("I want someone who will make me laugh at the littlest thing.") We clicked her preferences (fish and dogs are the best pets) and uploaded seven smiley, PG-rated photos with nothing more risqué than an exposed shoulder or two.

At 8 P.M. on a Wednesday, a couple of hours after Michelle had gone home, her profile was approved and popped up online. I'd been anxious about this. What if it went unnoticed for weeks, gathering dust in an obscure corner of the Internet?

No need to worry. Her profile was viewed within the first three minutes. Then again a minute later. The page-view counter shot up to eight, fourteen, twenty. Not quite Huffington Post numbers but brisk traffic. And then the e-mails started pinging in. A good dozen before I went to bed. I know that technically these guys aren't e-mailing me. Still, it's an exhilarating feeling to be so desired, if only by proxy. (And mind you, I did type in the essay and clean up her grammar.)

:-D

"Hey baby, tell me you're coming to London," reads my first e-mail, from a British guy who works in advertising. Michelle has given me permission to reject the guys who are clearly wrong. An ocean qualifies as a deal breaker. I zap him back, "Sorry guvnor, no plans to come over there." I liked my response. Polite and firm—but a little flirty. I'm getting into character.

The next day, I show Michelle a half-dozen men with potential. The cute scientist with the Prince Charles ears, the guy from Long Island with eight siblings. We respond: "How are you?" "How was your week?" We keep it light, noncommittal—and short. That's an early lesson. I've always been the chaser, so I didn't realize quite how radically the balance of power shifts when you're the chasee. Michelle could have responded with a random string of letters and numbers, perhaps an umlaut and a backward slash, and these guys would be encouraged enough to ask her on a date.

After forty-five minutes of boyfriend shopping, Michelle leaves with my son for a trip to the museum. I spend an hour crafting personal rejection notes to yesterday's discard pile.

> Hello sexygentleman,
> Thanks for the email. I don't think we're quite the right match. But it was nice of you to contact me. Good luck in your search!

Then I type:

> By the way—just a friendly tip: The username sexygentleman might turn some women off. Maybe too on the nose.

Perhaps it isn't my place to say so. But, I figured, it is Michelle's. If a beautiful woman gave me advice—solid, well-intentioned advice—I'd pay attention.

Originally, I planned to send a personal ding letter to each of the unsuitable guys. But the volume is overwhelming. By day four, we've gotten close to fifty approaches. I'm starting to become shockingly picky. I have a growing list of instant deal breakers:

- If the guy uses the word *lady* or *ladies* in his opening e-mail
- If the guy lists his best feature as "butt" (ironically or not)
- If the guy uses more than two exclamation points in one sentence (One enthusiast wrote: "Hello there beautiful!!!!!!!!!!!!!")
- If the guy misspells the first word of his introductory essay. ("Chemestry is important.") I don't want to be a spelling snob, but the first word?
- If the guy's opening photo features a shot in which his head is tilted more than 20 degrees to the left or right
- If the guy has a photo of his Jet-Ski or snowmobile on his page

- If the guy is wearing sunglasses, any hat besides a baseball cap, or is bare-chested in his main photo
- If the guy refers to female anatomy anywhere in his initial correspondence (e.g., "I'm not a professional gynecologist, but, uh, I'd be happy to take a look")

Never in my life have I had such power. It's tremendous. Yes, at first I feel guilty about failing to respond to 70 percent of these guys. But it's just not possible. And in a way, it makes me feel better about my life as a single man. Maybe when my calls to beautiful women went unreturned, it wasn't because I was hideous or the women were evil. It was just a matter of time management.

;-)

I am rooting for one guy. He's got a warm, unforced smile, and he's humble, but not falsely humble. "I'm a geek, but a cool geek because I use a Mac," he writes. Unfortunately, Michelle rejects him. He's a drummer and music teacher. Her last boyfriend was a musician. She's sworn off them.

Michelle and I respond to a lot of the e-mails together. But just as often, she tells me to go ahead and reply myself while she's away. It's an amazing ego massage, sending e-mails as a beautiful woman. It's so easy. I type one moderately witty thing—not even moderately witty—and suddenly I'm Stephen Colbert. I told one guy that Michelle/I hang out at the Museum of Natural History, where there are "more nannies per square inch than any other place in America," and he responded that he was laughing uncontrollably at work. He said Michelle is "funny, intelligent, caring AND gorgeous."

It's not always adulation, though. A few suitors take a

snotty tone. One writes that he wants to know more about Michelle but adds, "I can tell from your profile that sometimes you're a handful."

That's annoying.

I respond: "What gives you the idea that I'm sometimes a handful?"

He responds: "I am so right!"

Now the bastard has really pissed me off. I click on his profile. A John Turturro look-alike with a smug smile. His opening photo shows him with his arm around a pretty woman with large breasts, as if to say, "I hang around with hot, large-breasted women, so if you are a hot, large-breasted woman, you should also hang around with me." He likes to "work hard and play harder." He is "VERY spiritual."

Michelle is not a handful. In her profile, she says that she's very open and will let you know when she's upset. That makes her a handful?

But I have a theory. I think the son of a bitch is employing an underhanded strategy. I edited an article a couple of years ago about a book called *The Game,* by Neil Strauss. It's about a nebbishy guy who decides to become the world's greatest pickup artist, and it became exceedingly popular with a certain type of single man. One major strategy Strauss talks about is to mildly insult a beautiful woman, lower her self-esteem, thus making her more vulnerable to your advances.

So I e-mail Handful Guy as Michelle: "Have you read The Game by Neil Strauss?"

He says, "What makes you ask me that?"

Yes! Busted.

I respond: "I was wondering if your first email was a neg." A "neg" is pickup patois for the mild insult.

He shoots back: "No, it was playful teasing. And yes, I have read the book."

Thus commences a flurry of e-mails arguing whether his line qualifies as a neg. Finally, he brings out his trump card: "Considering that I know most of the people in the book personally from before the book was released, I'm gonna have to disagree."

Aha. I hit the sleazeball jackpot, a longtime pickup artist. I tell him I'm glad my womanly radar warned me against him.

He says, "I was hoping online dating would introduce me to different girls than the ones I pick up and seduce in bars, clubs and starbucks. So far not."

It was the closest thing to an admission of guilt that I was going to get.

I write, "Just remember as you wade through the dating pool [his lame metaphor, by the way]: we women are not just here to be conquered as part of the game."

I'm a magnet for scammers. Everyone wants down my pants. Michelle probably would have sniffed this guy out eventually, but I'm proud that I saved her from a date.

☹

I was actually prepared for the scammers and the swagger. What I didn't expect was many men's tragic vulnerability when faced with a dazzling woman. One guy frets that his eyes look weird in his photos because he tried to blacken out the red-eye from the camera. He just wants Michelle to know they aren't that weird in real life.

A martial-arts enthusiast admits flat out that he's not worthy of Michelle but wants to let her know that "you are gorgeous."

A forty-one-year-old classical musician writes, "Not being striking in the looks department, I am someone who needs a chance to show his intellect and soul. And I realize how hard that will be when the first impression is made by pictures and written words, but I most sincerely hope you will give me the benefit of the doubt." You want to take these guys out for a milk shake. Or sign them up for Tony Robbins. Michelle and I send them encouraging notes: "You are a bit out of my age range, so I don't think it will work out. But I think you're a nice-looking gentleman."

Still, it's rejection, and a lot of men take it hard. "Never will we share a malbec overlooking the Rio at Córdoba in Argentina," writes one Harley-riding architect. "Never will we stand together in Amsterdam looking at Vermeer's Woman Pouring Milk. Never will I hold your hand. Never will I look into your eyes. Never will you look into mine."

A bit over-the-top, but I know what he's saying. I will never hold Michelle's hand, either, aside from in a game of ring-around-the-rosy.

The power of a beautiful woman's words is beginning to scare me. One guy begins his introductory essay, "When I was a child, I witnessed a clown jump to his death from a seven-story building. It was the only time a clown has made me laugh."

So I write him back on behalf of Michelle: "You're funny, but too dark for a sweet girl like me." Both of which are true.

"Just tell me I'm ugly," he said.

A few days later, he changed his profile to an essay about his love of Care Bears and snuggling. Yes, it was a joke, but there was an underlying sense of despair. He e-mailed Michelle that he really wanted to meet her. He needs a sweet girl. His revamped profile is only for her: "I made it in response to you."

Men will do anything for you.

;)

Michelle has her first off-line date tonight, and I'm freaking out. It's with the scientist guy who wears a lot of Patagonia jackets in his photos. I keep staring at my cell phone, jittery as a dad with a daughter going to the prom. Forty minutes after their scheduled meeting time, Michelle text-messages me from the Starbucks where they were supposed to get together. He never showed up. "That's it for me and online dating," she writes. "It really isn't for me."

She's surprisingly sensitive. She should have Trump-like self-esteem, but she gets stood up once and she quits the game.

I'm furious at this Ph.D. bonehead. I spend an hour tracking down his real name on the Internet. (I know his alma mater and his specialty in marine biology.) I consider showing up outside his office and asking him why he's got the emotional maturity of a third grader. Do you know what you've just blown, you idiot? Plus, in one of his e-mails, the guy said he didn't like pancakes. What kind of asshole doesn't like pancakes?

Then I just get depressed and insecure. What did we say that made him blow us off? It wasn't her looks. So it must have been our banter. Did we not talk enough about reef decay in Honduras? Dammit. My walk on the feminine side is over. My vicarious single life is dead.

The next day, the scientist e-mails. He was actually at the Starbucks. He was waiting outside. And Michelle, it turns out, was waiting inside. Come on! This guy can't even find a beautiful woman in a Starbucks the size of your average living room.

But Michelle and I are both relieved. She agrees to try again. I make another plea with her to give the smiley rocker a chance. I had e-mailed him that "I had a bad experience with musicians." He had shot back that he's "NOT" that guy. He's been sending us long e-mails about his family, his career, and the magnificence of xylophones. He apologizes for the length, but "they just flow out of me." I don't mind. Most of these guys are too lazy to form a complete thought. A rambling e-mail is better than "u a hottie."

Michelle says she'll think about it.

∴

:0

Today I get the most startling e-mail yet. It's from a guy with the screen name "watchmeontelevision." Who could it be? Goran Visnjic? Al Roker?

I open it up. "I must confess that I am currently involved with someone but quite frankly am looking for a girl on the side. . . .

"As you noticed I have no photo to share but I periodically represent my company on national TV. I'll be on [show you've never heard of on a minor cable network]. My name is [his full name here].

"I suppose on your path to finding Mr. Right I could perhaps be Mr. Right Now. . . ."

Oh boy. Did he really use the "Mr. Right Now" line? And is he actually trying to leverage his two minutes on an obscure cable network show into sex with a hot mistress? And why did the subject line say "renaissance woman"? Is that a new euphemism for slut?

I know I should have left it there. But I couldn't.

Me: "Intriguing. What's it like to be on TV?"

He asks me to watch him and tell him what I think. So I TiVo it. Afterward, I e-mail to ask if he was flirting with the host. He responds with a cocky e-mail about how the host isn't his type—but "you seem like you might be my type."

I shoot back that I'm not sure it's a good idea: "I feel a bit guilty about borrowing another woman's man. Do you feel guilty?"

I was hoping to see a hint of remorse, something to humanize him.

He responds: "You know how they say the forbidden fruit is always the best."

Nope. No remorse. I tell him again that I'm conflicted.

He says meet him this afternoon for a drink, and one of two

things will happen: I'll feel uncomfortable, or I'll want to meet him later for a nightcap.

I say maybe, but let's keep e-mailing. We chat about travel and our favorite foods. I ask him about the craziest thing he's ever done.

"Being a business guy who's ballsy enough to try to be on television, contemplating running for political office"—wait, did he just say he was contemplating running for political office?—"moving to ten states for my job, romantic fantasies. (oh, that one slipped out—do you have any fantasies?)"

Uh-oh. Here we go. There's no way I can show this to Michelle. She would be mortified.

I should just drop it, but I don't. Why?

To teach this cretin a lesson?

Because I'm drunk with power? I'm a beautiful woman. I can make these miscreants do anything I want.

Revenge? Against men who give our gender a bad name?

Whatever it is, it's something male. I want to take him down.

I respond, "I think food and sex make a nice combo LOL. Some whipped cream. Cherries. Maybe some chocolate syrup."

I just want to open the door, not get too graphic.

TV guy says, "I like your fantasies involving food and sex. . . . My fantasies are a bit more risque than that, so maybe I should hold off until you know me better."

I write, "Send them to me. Nothing can shock me."

A total setup.

He writes back, "Let's start with the tamest version of my most common fantasy—taking you to a strip club on amateur night (although there is nothing amateur about your photos!). I'd like to see you strip for other men, and as we're entering the club you have on a long fur coat and you're wearing stiletto heels, but underneath the coat I know you've got on little else . . ."

It's a well-crafted, highly detailed account that stretches a good two pages.

". . . You walk out onstage wearing a lacy black bra from which your breasts are spilling out. You have on a black thong. . . . You rip off your bra and thong, and your gorgeous, naked body is out there for all to see . . ."

It continues with an increasingly graphic description of things she does to the audience. Then he concludes: ". . . if you'd like to continue the fantasy by telling me how you'd react . . ."

Okay. This has gone into unsettling territory. I have to end it. I take the offensive.

"I found your fantasy disturbing on many levels. It made me feel dirty, but not in a good way. I felt like you were exhibiting me to other men like a piece of meat. I am not a piece of meat. I am not a prostitute. . . . I know famous people get away with a lot because of their fame. But I think its best if we end our conversations here."

I feel momentarily gleeful about punishing this guy. Though more than a bit like a manipulative bastard in my own right.

As it happens, I have been having a simultaneous e-mail exchange with another sketchy character. This is a guy who, in his opening e-mail, said he was a "BAD boy." Capitalized. I ask him what makes him bad. He says he'll do things that would take my breath away. I ask him for details.

He writes "after the nice dinner and the club . . . and after turning u on with my nice attitude and sexy thoughts, we will rush to my place where I'll begin by kissing ur sexy lips . . . kissing my way down your stomach . . . and then your inner thighs . . . [detailed description here of the licking] also . . . i really want to see more photos."

I write back: "I'm afraid there's been a terrible misunderstanding. When I said I wanted details of how you'd take my breath away, I meant details such as the type of flowers you'd send me, the candlelit restaurant you'd take me to, et cetera."

He responds: "it all started with a dinner and a night at the club. i just didn't give u details about how romantic the dinner was. . . . no photo?"

This guy is wonderfully oblivious. As if he'd only thrown in a description of the tablecloth before the graphic licking it would have been okay.

But that's it. No more of this nonsense. No more setting guys up and then smacking them down, even if they are cheaters. This is wrong. What am I? Fourteen? Or Chris Hansen from *Dateline*? I can't be wasting my time on this stuff when I have to find Michelle a boyfriend.

I feel guilty enough to write a softening note to the TV guy— who had apologized for making me feel dirty. I write that I over-reacted but added that I still couldn't bring myself to cheat with him. I send it off. Then I noticed I signed the note "A.J." Damn! I am dumb. I'm dumber than an aspiring politician who sends dirty e-mail fantasies over the Internet. A week or so later, he e-mails Michelle again. He addresses her as "A.J." and begs her to "come out an play." I don't respond.

:-)

Michelle has another off-line date, and this time I make sure to tell him to meet her inside the bar. It's the smiley, shaggy-haired rocker. She's giving him a chance.

In a last-minute panic attack out of *Three's Company,* I call Michelle to tell her she should say she went to a Super Bowl party last week. I had e-mailed the rocker to tell him how much fun the party was before I found out Michelle got sick and had skipped it in real life.

Again, I wait with my cell phone in hand for the postdate update.

"It was pretty good," she says.

"Just pretty good?"

"It was great. He's very sweet."

I feel giddy enough to do an actual fist pump. I'm investing a lot in this guy. He's my discovery. He's my stand-in.

I had been worried that Michelle's online personality would be too different from the way she acts in real life. She's usually much shyer than the hybrid we've created. What if he suspects something fishy? But no, Michelle told me she actually made herself act less shy to conform to her online self.

"When I got there, he said, 'What do you think?' And I made him turn around in a circle before I said, 'Not bad.' "

I'm psyched. I'm Henry friggin' Higgins. Michelle doesn't yet know if the chemistry is there, but the rocker is definitely worth a second date.

I hang up, and my giddiness soon wears off. It's replaced by sadness. A weird sadness. Almost melancholy, like something out of a Goethe novel. I realize it's because I'm vicariously experiencing the feelings of a crush, the excitement, the possibility, both on Michelle's part and the rocker's.

I'd forgotten that feeling. And it's bittersweet, because I know that I can't experience that sensation firsthand. I love being married—I love its depth and comfort—but I miss the crush. Unless you happen to be Mr. watchmeontelevision, you don't get to feel the rush of the crush. I'm jealous of the long-haired rocker.

:-\

The next day, Michelle pulls up a chair to my computer to go over that day's haul with me. A whole bunch of e-mails. One cheeseball has written, "I know that you probably get tons of e-mails from dudes trying to use coy pickup lines. But I don't care about that. I wanna know if you're beautiful on the inside."

I've gotten more believable e-mails from Nigerian barristers. But he's right about one thing: she gets lots of dudes complimenting her on her looks. Her pretty eyes, pretty smile, pretty dimples. She's been called the entire "attractive" entry of the thesaurus: "captivating," "luminescent," "radiant."

"How many of them do you think read the profile?" Michelle asks me. I laugh and turn to look at her. She keeps her eyes on the screen.

We click on a thirty-four-year-old who describes his job as international investigator for a corporation—whatever that means. Michelle looks at his photo.

"If we have kids, they'll have huge chins," she says.

"Why?"

"Because I have a big chin," she says. I stare at her chin. It's not big. It's not even half the size of Reese Witherspoon's. Now, I'm sure *Redbook* has run a thousand articles about how even Gisele has insecurities about her body. But beautiful women don't confess it to men so much. Maybe Michelle is starting to see me as a fellow woman. Disturbing.

The chin issue notwithstanding, a couple of days later Michelle goes on a date with the international investigator. I get the cell phone call.

"How'd it go?"

"It was just okay."

That's Michelle's equivalent of "disastrous." A date with Muqtada al-Sadr would be "just okay."

"What happened?"

"I was really self-conscious," she says. "He stared at me the whole time. I couldn't even look him in the eyes."

The next night, a second date with the rocker, at a Thai restaurant. I wait for the call. It comes too early, just ninety minutes after the date.

"He's nice, but there's no chemistry, I think."

I'm crushed. I thought there was a chance. I can help her write the notes, I can pick the guys, but I can't control that damn chemistry.

Maybe she'll find some chemistry with Ted from Long Island, the one with eight siblings. He's scheduled for next week. And so is "Loveable Hal."

I know she'll find it with someone. Not just because the e-mails from interested men keep flooding in, unabated. But because of the men themselves. The only thing more surprising than the quantity and deviousness of the creeps is the emotional honesty and fragility of the noncreeps. It's a side of men that other men just don't get to see.

It's enough to bring out the nurturer in anybody. Which is why I log on to the dating service and do a search for "depressed" and another one for "lonely." I find this:

ummmm, I just turned 28. Sorry to say I still live at home with my mother. Shes getting old and I help her out. I have NO LIFE. Go to work and come home, and play video games.

The next day, Michelle and I write him a note: "I just wanted to say that I think it's great that you take care of your mom. There aren't enough nice guys in this world. I don't think we're right for each other (I don't believe in long-distance relationships), but I think you'll be a catch for some lucky girl."

Well, it's something. To paraphrase another guy with a double identity, with great beauty comes great responsibility.

CODA

A few weeks later, Michelle dumped me. She let me down easy—
"I think maybe I need a break from Internet dating," she said.
But I knew what that meant. I was getting the boot. I was no
longer her Cyrano.

I tried to convince her to give it another shot. But when
we logged on and saw a note from screen name "Violentbunny,"
that was it. She was finished for good. (Violentbunny: you, sexy-
gentleman, and Topnotchlover need to have a good brainstorming
session.)

Michelle said she'd just wait and hope that love came to her.
Which I thought was a terrible idea. But it actually did. Six
months later, she started dating an old friend she knew from
when she worked at a Washington, D.C., hotel. They're still
together.

I wish I'd been the one to find her love. But Michelle told me
that I helped. I got her back into the dating mind-set, back to
thinking about relationships. Without her great Internet Dating
Adventure, she says, she'd still be single and lonely. I hope she's
telling the truth.

Regardless, my dating career is over for now. I've got mixed
feelings. Being a beautiful woman had its perks. The nonstop
positive attention comes to mind. But it was also an emotionally
draining experience. The amount of rejecting I had to do was
mind-boggling. Every day it was "no, no, nope, no thanks, no."
And not just to the sleazy guys. Sometimes to kind, vulnerable
men. Type the wrong thing and you'll send these fellows into a
tailspin. I never before thought of the built-in guilt that comes
with having a pretty face.

It was draining, too, trying to suss out the schemers. There
were a huge number of people out there pretending to be what

they aren't. Including me, of course. (Incidentally, a colleague of mine goes into Internet poker rooms and pretends to be a woman, because he says his opponents assume women are worse at poker. I can't decide whether taking advantage of sexist stereotypes is ethically acceptable.) There's a lot of deceit, boasting, and creepiness that you'll find in Internet dating.

But the semi-anonymity of the Internet also makes it an honesty amplifier. Men will open themselves right up, laying bare their fears, insecurities, and hopes. My months of e-dating convinced me there are plenty of mensches out there. Or maybe they're just sleazy guys who had their sensitive sisters write notes for them.

$$\text{Fame} \leq \text{Ego}(x)^3$$

$$\frac{\text{Zen} + \text{Focus} = \text{Productivity}^2}{\sqrt{\text{Brain} \cdot \text{Caveman}}} = \frac{1}{x}$$

$$\frac{\text{Outsourcing}^8 + \text{marriage}}{12,000 \text{ miles}} = 9$$

$$x = \frac{\text{Nudity} + \text{Public}}{\text{Dignity}}$$

$$\sqrt{\frac{\text{Nudity} + \text{Public}}{\text{Dignity}}}$$

$$(\text{Geo. Wash.} - \text{wig})\,\text{Me} = x$$

$$\frac{\text{Dating} + \text{Beauty}}{x(\text{Cyrano})} \neq \text{Love}$$

$$\int_b^a \frac{\text{husband}}{(\text{wife})\text{power}}$$

$$(\text{wife})\text{power}^3 = x$$

$$\frac{\text{Reason} - \text{Emotion}}{\text{Behavior}} = \text{Insanity}$$

$$\text{Truth}^n - \text{filter} = \text{Chaos}$$

Chapter Nine

Whipped

The most common theme of the e-mails I get sent—with the possible exception of Canadians who are furious that I misspelled Wayne Gretzky's name in my first book (who knew Canadians could get so worked up?)—is that my wife is a saint.

These e-mails are sent by readers who are in awe of Julie for putting up with my biblical beard, or for tolerating the endless stream of facts about, say, China's opium wars during my year of reading the *Britannica*. And all the other general nonsense that comes with my projects. Often, they'll say that I owe her something for the suffering I've inflicted—precious stones, perhaps.

But a handful of readers have suggested that diamond earrings aren't enough. I need to pay Julie back in a more appropriate fashion. I need to spend a month doing everything my wife says. She will be boss. I will be her devoted servant. It will be a month, they say, of foot massages and talking about feelings and scrubbing dishes and watching Kate Hudson movies (well, if Julie actually liked Kate Hudson movies, which she doesn't).

I've laughed off the idea for a couple of years now. I won't argue with the thesis that Julie's a saint. But the experiment is . . . well, if I'm being honest, it's actually a pretty good idea. It does seem a suitable way to end this year of human guinea pigging, the honorable thing to do for my wife. Plus, it could be revelatory. It'll let me explore the tricky power dynamics of the modern American marriage. It'll allow me to study the Mars/Venus, *Everybody Loves Raymond* clichés about gender battles and figure out which are true and which are hogwash.

When I told Julie about Operation Ideal Husband (or Operation Whipped, as my friend John calls it), she jumped for joy. I'm not speaking metaphorically. She bounded around the living room on an invisible pogo stick, clapping her hands and saying "Yay!"

When I told my friends, they all had the same joke: You're going to do everything your wife says for a month? How is that different from every other month in the last eight years?

Yeah, yeah. It's true. Julie is, in some ways, already the CEO of our family. Since I put her through such misery with my experiments, I tend to defer to her on most other matters—travel, food, clothes. Especially clothes.

I'm a terrible dresser. My only two criteria for clothes are that they be soft and loose-fitting. One of Julie's favorite jokes is to give me a dollar when I'm looking particularly disheveled. You know, like I'm a hobo.

She got so disturbed by my fashion blindness, she spent an afternoon rearranging my closet. It now has three sections, each with a black-and-white printed label taped to the shelf.

Clothes to Wear Only at Home (my sixteen-year-old Brown
     University sweatshirt, for instance)
Clothes for Both Home and Outside (anything with a Banana Republic label)
Clothes That Require Permission to Wear (anything purchased at Saks)

Yes, I have to ask my wife's permission to wear my nice sweaters. Lucky for her, they usually are too snug for my tastes, so I rarely have the urge.

So to use a clothing metaphor, Julie generally wears the pants in the family. But this month, I'll be washing those pants and ironing them. I'll be geishalike in my obedience. I'll think of nothing but her happiness. I'll take over her chores. I'll be like an obedient eighteenth-century wife to my twenty-first-century wife.

I should make a confession, though: part of my plan is to be so compliant, she'll see that that's not what she wants. She'll learn to appreciate my occasionally insubordinate pain-in-the-ass self. That was the plan, anyway.

GROUNDWORK

A couple of days before I start, I ask Julie to tell me some things she wants from me during this month. She lays down *Gone With the Wind*—which she's been reading for the last two months—and starts to talk. It's a good thing I brought a notebook.

"Well, let's start with the bed. No forcing me to the edge of the bed with your six pillows.

"No waking me up when you come in at night by using your BlackBerry as a flashlight and shining it in my face.

"And movies. No talking during movies.

"No looking over at me during sad parts of movies to see if I'm crying."

I'm scribbling away, trying to keep up. It's kind of disturbing how easily this river of minor grievances flows out of Julie. One after another, without a pause, pinballing from one topic to another.

"No buying the first fruit you pick up at the grocery store.

"No wasting food. If the boys don't finish something, wrap it up and keep it for the next meal.

"No leaving books in random piles around the apartment."

She was in the zone. I have pet peeves, too, but I don't think I could recall them with such accuracy and speed. It's at once impressive and disturbing.

"No making fun of my family.

"No complaining about having to go to D.C. to visit Henry and Jennifer every year.

"If I ask a simple question like 'Is the drugstore open on Sundays?' and you don't know the answer, try saying 'I don't know.' Do not say 'It's a mystery that humans have been pondering for centuries, but scientists and philosophers are no closer to an answer.' "

Fair enough. I can see how that might get old.

"Go to sleep at a decent hour so you're not a zombie in the morning.

"Be more knowledgeable about our finances.

"No hovering over my shoulder and reading my *US Weekly* and then claiming you're not interested in that stuff.

"No putting things back in the fridge when there's just a teensy, tiny bit left."

"Wait a second," I say. "You just said, 'Don't waste food.' I'm getting mixed messages here."

"It's a fine line, but I think you can figure it out."

It went on and on, this list. What's happening here? Has the power already gone to her head? Or am I unusually difficult to live with?

I must have looked like I just got beaned by an Olympic shot put to the forehead, because Julie softened.

"I love you," she says.

"Noted," I say.

THE FIRST DAY

"Good morning, honey! You look terrific!"

I'm really playing it up.

"Thanks, sweetie!" She's playing right back to me.

Soon after, she assigns me my first chore.

"Can you think of a third gift we can give your father for his birthday?"

Three gifts? That was my initial reaction. My reflex was to make some lame remark, like "Three gifts? Two aren't enough? What, was he born in a manger?" Instead I said, "Sure."

This is something I notice throughout the day. Whenever Julie says something, my default setting is to argue with her. It's (usually) not overtly hostile bickering. It's just affectionate parrying. Verbal jujitsu.

But at the same time, I know it's not good. You playfully bicker enough, and after a few years, it stops becoming playful. Am I on the way to becoming the short, bald guy from the Lockhorns?

I've got to reboot my brain. I've got to stop seeing conversation as a series of offensive and defensive moves. Marriage isn't a zero-sum game. It doesn't have to be boxing. Maybe it can be two people with badminton racquets trying to keep the birdie in the air.

I spend the day trying to suppress my me-first instincts. Every decision, I ask: What would Julie want? I start to cut the cantaloupe for my sons' breakfast, and stop. Julie once complained that I cut cantaloupes all jagged, like a graph of the

NASDAQ. I couldn't care less, but it matters to her. So, a sharper knife and a smooth and straight cut.

Frankly, it's exhausting to check with my inner Julie every twenty seconds.

"You liking this?" I ask.

"Loving it. And it's great for our marriage. Right?"

"Right!"

The apartment's chilly, so Julie slides her hands under my shirt to warm them up. One of my least favorite of her habits. Two Popsicles on my stomach. I bite my tongue.

HENPECKING THROUGH HISTORY

If I'd tried this experiment a couple of hundred years ago, I'd be breaking the law.

Stephanie Coontz writes in her great book *Marriage, a History*, that if the wife wore the pants in a family, the husband wasn't just an object of contempt—he was a criminal. "A husband could be fined or ducked in the village pond for not controlling his wife." In Colonial America, men sometimes "sued for slander if neighbors gossiped that a husband was allowing his wife to usurp his authority."

In the Middle Ages, rural villages had a charming ritual called charivaris for those who didn't discipline their wives: "A henpecked man might be strapped to a cart or ridden around backward on a mule, to be booed and ridiculed for his inversion of the accepted marital hierarchy."

Coontz makes clear what I already suspected: For most of history, marriage was wildly undemocratic. Husband and wife were like czar and peasant, chairman of the board and receptionist.

In fact, wifely obedience was pretty much synonymous with

marriage. Confucius defined a wife as "one who submits to another." Coontz writes that ancient Romans opposed gay marriage not because of homosexuality, which they had no problem with, but because "no real man would ever agree to play the subordinate role demanded of a Roman wife."

Throughout most of history, I'd be seen as a traitor to my gender. I should instead learn some marital tips from, say, Scottish poet Robert Burns. In his 1788 poem "The Henpecked Husband," he writes:

> Curs'd be the man, the poorest wretch in life,
> The crouching vassal to a tyrant wife!
> Who has no will but by her high permission,
> Who has not sixpence but in her possession;
> Who must to he, his dear friend's secrets tell,
> Who dreads a curtain lecture worse than hell.
> Were such the wife had fallen to my part,
> I'd break her spirit or I'd break her heart;
> I'd charm her with the magic of a switch,
> I'd kiss her maids, and kick the perverse bitch.

Lovely, right?

I call Coontz to see if she knows of any cultures—past or present—in which women reigned supreme. The short answer: no. There's never been a true matriarchal society, not counting the legendary single-nippled Amazons. There have been matrilineal societies—in southern India, among Native Americans in New Jersey—where descent is traced through the woman. Coontz is partial to such societies, but they are very rare. "Matrilineal societies tend to be more peaceful and inclusive," she says.

I tell Julie about my research and read her the Robert Burns poem.

"See? You're very lucky you weren't Robert Burns's wife."

"Yes. Very lucky. But you're not allowed to do that this month."

"What?"

"Compare yourself to other husbands."

It's true. I'm a shameless comparer. It's a reflex born of insecurity. Any time I hear about a husband behaving badly, I can hardly wait to tell Julie. See? You're lucky I don't have affairs with my coworkers. See? You're lucky I don't work till eleven every night. See? You're lucky I don't lock our kids in the basement and create a second secret family like that Austrian guy.

Julie put such comparisons on her thou-shalt-not list, though she sometimes breaks the rule herself. Last week, she sent me an e-mail that said "YOU are lucky" followed by the Fox News headline WOMAN SHOOTS BOYFRIEND FOR NOT LETTING HER SLEEP. Julie, you might have guessed, loves her sleep.

IT IS BETTER TO GIVE

One of Julie's guidelines for Project Ideal Husband is, naturally, for me to buy her flowers. I object that we're in the middle of a fierce recession (I know—not very obedient of me). Flowers in New York are so astonishingly expensive, I can only surmise that they are kept hydrated with water drawn from the fjords of Norway by specially trained geologists.

"It doesn't have to be flowers," Julie says. "Gifts of any kind will do."

When we started dating, I was a decent gift giver. I gave Julie books and soaps and cinnamon-scented candles. Then the presents slowly trailed off. Maybe my gift-giving deficiency is genetic. My dad is still living down the gift he gave my mom for their first Valentine's together: nothing.

The reasoning: If he got my mom something fancy, and then one year down the road, he forgot to get her anything, she'd think he loved her less. He didn't want her to think that. So the best way to prevent that situation was not to get her anything at all.

Which is actually quite rational, in its own way.

Going against family tradition, I've started to bring Julie a gift a day. Mostly, no-foam lattes. But also DVDs and soaps and books.

I'm starting to plan these gifts days in advance. I look forward to seeing Julie's smile when I set them on her desk. I haven't gotten any jumping for joy again, but she did rub her hands with glee when I gave her the autobiography of Maureen McCormick, who played Marcia Brady before descending into cocaine addiction (Julie's a fan of the Bradys *and* addiction memoirs).

The Bible's "it's better to give than receive" was not the raving of a lunatic. It goes back to a recurring theme I've found in almost all my experiments: behavior shapes your thoughts.

My brain sees me giving a gift to Julie.

My brain concludes I must really love her.

I love her all the more. Which means I'm happier in my relationship, if a bit poorer.

MR. MOM, THE SEQUEL

I rented *Mr. Mom* the other day, the early 1980s movie. It's the one with Michael Keaton getting fired and having to stay at home with the kids (best line from Keaton: "I'm a regular Phil Donahue!"). Every joke has the exact same premise: man attempts to use household appliance, household appliance goes berserk and sends off sparks. The domicile is a foreign and scary land to the 1983 male.

But things must be better in our enlightened twenty-first century, right? Actually, no. According to a recent *New York Times Magazine* cover story, women on average still do twice as much housework as men, about 31 hours to 14 hours. And here's the strange part: that ratio holds mostly true *even if both spouses have full-time jobs*. Even worse for women is the child-care ratio. Moms do an average of five times as much with the kids as dads. (Working moms do a measly 3.7 times as much.) This is the same ratio as ninety years ago.

It wasn't always this way. Once upon a time, housecleaning was seen as macho. Or at least it wasn't unmanly. Back in the Middle Ages, when the husband and wife both worked at home making candles and barrels and whatnot, "domesticity was a virtue shared by males and females, a shorthand term for thrift, hard work and order," writes Coontz. Then in the Industrial Revolution, men went to work outside the home, and "domesticity tumbled out of the constellation of masculine virtues." Women's work became devalued, "seen as an act of love, rather than a contribution to survival."

If we're looking at it with cold Spock-like rationality, then, as the *Times* says, "gender should not determine the division of labor" in the home.

I'd always figured I was a regular Phil Donahue. I did my fair share of housework—or at least more than the average guy. But just to make sure, I asked Julie to list all the household chores she does.

"I clean up the kids' rooms. I set up playdates for our kids. I take them to doctor's appointments. I pay the bills. I get the baby gifts for my friends . . ."

If this were a movie, it would show clock hands spinning around, maybe calendar days flipping by. What I'm saying is, it's a long freakin' list.

"I fill the liquid soap dispensers. I wash our placemats. I get new toner for the printer."

Julie paused. "This exercise may cause a lot of trouble for you."

I was thinking the same thing. She does chores I didn't even know existed.

"I'll do everything in the house for the month," I said.

"I can't let you do that," she says. Our apartment would look like Grey Gardens within two weeks.

The *Times Magazine* talked about something called Equal Parenting, also known as Peer Marriage or Symmetrical Marriage. It's a movement started by a feminist writer named Alix Kates Shulman in 1969, who drew up a famous twenty-two-point Marriage Agreement that split the duties ("Nighttime: Husband does Tuesday, Thursday and Sunday. Wife does Monday, Wednesday and Saturday . . . wife strips beds, husband remakes them."). Shulman and her husband later got divorced.

But our marriage can handle it, right? Just give me a bunch of tasks and I'll check them off.

The next morning, Julie says, "Okay, call the pediatrician and schedule Zane's—you know what? I'll just do it. It's faster."

This is the problem. Julie's just more competent at a lot of these tasks. Or all of them. She's the single most organized person in the world, a woman who not only subscribes to *Real Simple* magazine, but also fills the pages with color-coded tabs and labels and then archives them, next to her old *TV Guides*.

Maybe that's why women do more housework. They're better at it. They were born with the tidiness gene. I call Helen

Fisher, an anthropologist who specializes in genetic gender differences hoping she'll confirm my hunch. No luck. She tells me I can't blame my laziness on my Y chromosome.

Okay, then. If Michael Keaton can tame a vacuum cleaner, then I can master this domestic stuff, too. I've decided the key is to be aggressive, "proactive" as they used to say in business meetings. I have to be an alpha househusband.

My friend Albert e-mails. He works on a cable TV drama starring Timothy Hutton, and his first episode is airing in two weeks.

I type an e-mail to Julie: "Should we record it?"

Before I press SEND, I pause.

The "we" in that sentence? It's actually "Julie." The true meaning of my e-mail: "Julie, would you record it?"

I delete the e-mail. I schlep into the living room and program the TiVo myself.

Yeah, I know. I'm a hero. But there are dozens, hundreds of little chores calling out to be done. I'm overwhelmed. I spend two hours writing and the rest of the day reattaching knobs to cabinets and putting stray CDs in containers. To paraphrase the title of a bestselling book about modern-day women, I don't know how the hell does Julie do it.

THE PERILS OF NICENESS

I'm suffering from a disease. At least if you believe Seattle-based therapist Robert Glover. He thinks millions of American men are afflicted with something called Nice Guy Syndrome. And he's here to cure us.

He talks to me from his parked car in Bellevue, Washington. The obvious question: What's wrong with being a nice guy? Well, his definition of a nice guy is being a yes-man to your wife.

"First, it's inherently dishonest," he says. "Your wife doesn't really know what you think, feel, or want."

Second, Nice Guys might seem nice, but eventually the resentment builds up. "They give and give and give and eventually they'll explode and all the stuff will come out. I call it the Victim Puke."

Third, women don't really like it. As the saying goes, if you behave like a doormat, you'll get treated like a doormat.

A former evangelical preacher, Glover left the church following his divorce. His life shattered, he reinvented himself: he ingested the writings of Robert Bly and others, started workshops for men, and penned a book called *No More Mr. Nice Guy*.

According to Glover, Nice Guy Syndrome is reaching epidemic proportions. "Every generation of young men is becoming less masculine, and more passive and pleasing. Hell, I just think we have more estrogen in our drinking water."

So what's the alternative?

Be a man. "The metaphor is being the lead on the dance floor. Being clear and firm, making her look good and feel good. I grew up in the sixties and seventies, so when I say this, I still expect pink lightning to hit me, but women are security-seeking creatures. They want to trust. And if you mess with a woman's sense of trust, she'll never get wet."

If I continue to be the Nicest Guy in the World, he warns, I'll disappear as a human.

"I've seen this happen. Men forget what they like. I put a legal pad in front of them and say, 'What do you like to do,' and they literally just stare at this legal pad. They've forgotten to ask themselves, 'What would make *you* happy.' "

But Dr. Glover actually thinks my strategy is good. I'll overdose on Niceness. It's like when you're on a diet and you force six pieces of cheesecake down your maw until you're fully nauseated and won't crave cheesecake for a long, long time. I'll leave behind my cocoon of wussiness and emerge a man.

Oh, and Julie will get sick of me, too. "If you leave it all up to the woman, they get tired of that. They feel burdened. If a man leads, has a plan, and says, firmly, but with love, 'Let's go out and have pizza,' she can say, 'I don't want pizza. How about Mexican?' It gets the conversational ball rolling. . . . Women don't like people who kiss their ass."

After I hang up, I go into our bedroom and tell Julie that Dr. Glover says she'll get bored of being in total charge.

"Does he know me?"

SATISFYING THE WIFE'S APPETITES

In the 1780s, protofeminist Judith Sargent Murray made the radical suggestion: that men should help prepare meals, since men do at least half of the eating.

I know. The gall!

I've decided to implement Murray's crazy notion. I'm making Julie some chicken piccata—chicken with lemon juice, olive oil, and white wine. Julie comes into the kitchen when she hears the baffling sound of me pounding the chicken breasts with a rolling pin.

She looks surprised. Then skeptical.

"Is this going to be more work for me?" she asks.

"That's what you say to me when I'm making you dinner?"

"You're right," she says. "Thank you for making me dinner."

Since our twins were born, Julie rarely cooks aside from microwaved hot dogs and mac 'n' cheese. We adults in the family rely mostly on her color-coded binder of order-in menus.

My dinner does not result in any *Mr. Mom* wackiness. The

rice pilaf doesn't explode all over the kitchen walls. The chicken breasts don't send us to the hospital with botulism.

I light the candles, pour the wine, serve the chicken.

"No napkin over your arm?" asks Julie.

"Sorry."

Aside from the napkin oversight, I'd go so far as to say it's a little romantic.

"If you cook for me every night, we could have sex every night," Julie says.

"I don't want to have sex every night."

"I thought all men did."

"All men who are seventeen."

Which brings up a question. How often should the ideal husband have sex with his wife? The average married couple has sex just about twice a week, according to several recent surveys (a statistic probably skewed by the randy just-married twenty-two-year-olds).

Is that what the woman wants? Or is it some compromise? It's not clear.

I know from my biblical year that Jews consider it a husband's obligation to satisfy his wife. The Talmud has startlingly specific instructions on frequency. Namely:

A man of independent wealth is "obligated" to have sex with his wife every day
A donkey driver once a week
A camel driver once a month
A sailor once every six months
A scholar once a week, on the Sabbath

It's not clear whether the sages consulted women when drawing up this list.

I may not be an official scholar, but the once-a-week schedule sounds good. Especially for an unofficial scholar with three very loud children.

"How often is ideal for you?" I ask.

"Once a week sounds good, too." She pauses. "Please don't put that in the book."

"You'll read it and see how it looks on the page."

Incidentally, I recently read that Madonna had a "marriage contract" that ordered Guy Ritchie to devote time to the couple's "sexual expressiveness." He was also given words to say during an argument, including "I understand that my actions have upset you; please work with me to resolve this." Madonna allegedly taped the contract to the fridge, and if Guy broke the rules, she'd chide him, "Contract, contract!"

Like Madonna and Alix Kates Shulman, I'm not opposed to writing down some mutual guidelines for a partnership. But maybe including "sexual expressiveness" in there isn't the path to marital bliss.

EVERYBODY LOVES JULIE

We're late for a dinner date with her friends. I'm scouring the closet for my wool hat.

"Step it up," says Julie.

"Great idea!" I say, all chipper.

"We're late."

"Thanks for the motivation!"

That's my new strategy—exaggerated enthusiasm.

"I actually don't like this new 'great!' and 'super!' thing."

"Great! I'll have to work on that."

Calvin Trillin, in his wonderful tribute to his late wife, Al-ice, said that every writer portrays his or her family somewhere on the spectrum between sitcom and Lifetime movie. Julie's and mine is firmly in the sitcom genre. She's the sensible one, the straight man to my wacky schemes. She makes the realistic decisions, and I do what she says.

Our real marriage is like the one portrayed in my books, and yet it isn't. I overrepresent the conflict, for one thing. It's not that the conflict doesn't exist. The fights happen. But I don't write about the hours of peaceful, contented coexistence.

But here's the weird thing—I think the reality is starting to catch up with the writing. We're starting to act more and more like our characters from my books. We do the bantering with more frequency. She rolls her eyes more often at my antics.

I think this happens in every relationship, not just writers'. Each partner gets a label—the messy one, the neurotic one, the forgetful one—and then they start to live up to that label. That's what I've noticed in my experiments: almost everything in life is a self-fulfilling prophecy. Probably even believing in self-fulfilling prophecies is a self-fulfilling prophecy.

I call up Coontz to ask her about the classic sitcom setup where the woman is the foil for the man. Who's in charge? We all know it's not Raymond. It's Raymond's wife.

"I think it's a face-saving way to deal with the fact the men are actually dominant. I enjoy a show like *Everybody Loves Raymond,* but I don't see it as empowering to women. The women get their way, but in the little things. They give in on the big things. They can't decide where to live, but they get to decide what furniture to buy."

Just for the record, Julie decided where to live (I wanted a warmer climate) and also what furniture to buy.

THE CLICHÉ TRUTH-O-METER

While we're on the topic of Mars-Venus stereotypes, Julie and I go through a list to see how we stack up.

Cliché: Men leave the toilet seat up.

Not true. I put the seat down, and not just out of chivalry. Out of hygiene. As a mild OCD sufferer, I've always shut the toilet cover before flushing, for fear of unseen mist. Then, just a few weeks ago, I read a review of a book called *The Big Necessity*, a cultural history of the bathroom. That took things to a new level. It said—and here's a spoiler alert: very unpleasant information coming up—that "aiming a stream of urine at a toilet bowl sends a fine spray around the room . . . which leaves a chemical deposit on anything surrounding the urinal. It can also change the color of wallpaper." Oh man. The book said that there's a vogue among German men to sit down when they pee. So as a mini-experiment, I've been trying the German style for the last week or so. My wallpaper color looks stable, and, as Larry David once pointed out, you get a little time to read. Okay, moving on.

Cliché: Men hate chick flicks.

Actually, Julie and I both love chick flicks, up to a point (that point being *Must Love Dogs*). I just like watching happy couples interact—such a rarity in real life. In fact, I'd be satisfied to watch the first act of a romantic comedy (couple falls in love) and the third act (couples makes up) and skip that stressful second act where they have all those unpleasant conflicts and misunderstandings.

Cliché: **Women are wildly sentimental,**
men are emotionally repressed.

Sort of true. I repress my anger, especially since Project Rationality. But so does Julie. We both believe venting just makes us
angrier. Don't go to sleep angry? Are you kidding? That's the
best thing we ever figured out to do. It's like hitting a reset button. Julie wakes up fresh, I wake up calm, and we can talk about
the argument. Or not talk about it. That works, too.

As for the good emotions, Julie is certainly better at expressing joy than I am. But I'm working on it. And neither of us is as
good as our kids. Jasper, for one, is the only nonironic user of
the phrase "Yippee!"

Cliché: **Men like to stay at home and women like to go out.**

Absolutely. Julie's a connector, a three-dimensional Facebook.
I'm a hard-core homebody. I envy the 1970s Hugh Hefner, not
because of his daily sexual intercourse with buxom women, but
because he got to stay in his house wearing pajamas all the time.

POWER CORRUPTS

Abigail Adams wrote to her husband, John, begging him to
make America's laws friendly to women: "All men would be tyrants if they could."

I think she's right. I'm wondering if all women would be
tyrants as well, given the chance. We're twenty days in, and the
power is going to Julie's head.

Her requests are coming faster and more abruptly.

"Change the batteries in the kids' toys."

"Clean out coffee machine."

She has started snapping at me. Literally snapping. I try to ask her something while she is watching *Top Chef,* and she answers me with three snaps and a wave of the hand, sign language for "Get out of the room now."

She's e-mailing me daily to-do lists. One item on today's list is "Put four Diet Cokes and four beers (any kind) in the refrigerator."

I write back: "Thanks for allowing me to choose the brand of beer! You obviously have a lot of faith in my judgment!"

"You're welcome!"

You remember the Stanford Prison Experiment? Where a bunch of college students were chosen to pretend to be "guards" and a bunch were to play "inmates" for two weeks? And how alarmingly quickly the "guards" started to abuse their power and demean the "inmates"? And how the experiment spun so out of control, they had to shut it down after six days?

I think I've got a mini-prison experiment going on here.

"Can you turn up the volume?"

We're watching *The Bachelor,* her choice.

"You have the remote," I say.

"I know. But I want you to walk to the TV and turn up the volume."

I'm not supposed to argue with her. I pause, but don't get up.

"Come on. This is the best month of my life. Let me make the most of it."

I heave myself off my chair.

HOW TO TALK TO YOUR SPOUSE

The best marriage advice book I've read is a paperback called *How to Talk So Kids Will Listen & Listen So Kids Will Talk.*

As you might deduce from the title, it wasn't meant as a marriage advice book. But the techniques in this book are so brilliant, I use them in every human interaction I can, no matter the age of the conversant. It's a strategy that was working well until today.

The book was written by a pair of former New York City teachers, and their thesis is that we talk to kids all wrong. You can't argue with kids, and you shouldn't dismiss their complaints. The magic formula includes: listen, repeat what they say, label their emotions. The kids will figure out the solution themselves.

I started using it on Jasper, who would throw a tantrum about his brothers monopolizing the pieces to Mouse Trap. I listened, repeated what he said, and watched the screaming and tears magically subside.

It worked so well, I decided, why limit it to kids? My first time trying it on a grown-up was one morning at the deli. I was standing behind a guy who was trying unsuccessfully to make a call on his cell.

"Oh come on! I can't get a signal here? Dammit. This is New York."

He looked at me.

"No signal?" I say. "Here in New York?" (Repeat what they say.)

"It's not like we're in goddamn Wisconsin."

"Mmmm." (Listen. Make soothing noises.)

"We're not on a farm. It's New York, for God's sake," he said.

"That's frustrating," I say. (Label their emotions.)

He calmed down.

Any time I see an adult tantrum brewing, I go right to my guidelines. Like tonight, when I gave our nanny our Netflix DVD of *Man on Wire* for the night.

"You lent it to Michelle without asking me?"

"I lent it to Michelle." (Repeating.) "I'm sorry."

"I was going to watch it tonight."

"You were going to watch it? Tonight?"

"I'd planned this out for a couple of days."

"Mmm."

"This is the second time you've done this."

"I can see how that would be really annoying."

She paused.

"Do *not* talk to me like you talk to the boys."

Damn. She figured it out? Was I too obvious?

"Don't talk to you like I talk to the boys?" I asked.

"The tone. It's the tone you use with Jasper."

"That must be frustrating."

"Stop it!"

THE NEW BALL AND CHAIN

My friend suggested that since I'm letting Julie whip me in the metaphorical sense, I should let her whip me in the literal sense. I consider it. I even look at a website where you can hire a whipping tutor in leather thigh boots and a Teutonic hat. But I don't do it. I think it'd be uncomfortable for everyone concerned.

But at the bottom of the website, I do find an interesting link. It's for a product I'd never heard of till now: a chastity belt for men. It's marketed at women who want to keep their man under lock and key.

Hmm. Julie just might enjoy that.

I click on it (which will no doubt result in some interesting spam in the future). The "Chastity Belt for Men CB-3000" comes in three varieties—clear plastic, imitation wood grain, or the new army camouflage version, for those who prefer their penises to blend into the surrounding foliage. It's got rings and pins and a small brass lock. It's got a compartment for your johnson. It looks like a dirty version of Tinker Toys.

And it will save your marriage. Or so claim the effusive testimonials on the website.

A German man writes, "My feelings for my wife become more intense. I have to spoil and caress her even more."

A Florida guy says, "It is so ironic that your product comes from Nevada—it is because of my antics in your state that I now find myself encased wearing a male chastity device. Now my wife lets me go to Vegas with a smile and the security of knowing that she is my key holder. This product is much more effective than the marriage counseling; a must for any open-minded couple who is dealing with issues of infidelity and rebuilding trust."

Julie isn't particularly concerned with me cheating. I know this because she seems to be immune from the emotion of jealousy. God knows I try to make her jealous. I invited four ex-girlfriends to our wedding, and Julie didn't bat an eye. I'll tell her "Hey, look at this woman who asked to be my Facebook friend!" And I'll show her a college co-ed who has photos of herself sticking out her studded tongue. "Good for you!" Julie will say.

She's just enviably, wonderfully secure. She has better things to do with her time than be jealous of a hypothetical, never-gonna-happen fling. If I ever took action, well . . . I think she'd put on her Teutonic hat and thigh boots.

And yet, the CB-3000 seems perfect for Project Ideal Husband. Julie's already got control of my schedule, my mind, my speech. Now she can control my private parts.

The CB-3000 arrives from Vegas a few days later in a small brown package. Julie's out to dinner with friends, so I decide this would be a good time to try it on. Give Julie a pleasant surprise when she returns.

This is more difficult than it sounds. I study the instructions for three minutes, then spend twenty minutes stretching and shoving myself into various rings and tubes. It's like assembling a complex model airplane, though this model airplane can pinch your sensitive regions and make you scream. Which happens three times.

I click the brass lock closed and tuck the key into the back pocket of my jeans.

I sit at my computer, adjusting and readjusting till Julie finally walks through the door. This is an unedited transcript of our conversation.

"What time did Jasper go to sleep?" she asks.

"Six-thirty. He was very tired." I pause. "I got you a present."

I hand her the small silver key.

"The key to your heart?" she asks.

"Better," I say.

I drop my pants.

She looks down at the Rube Goldberg contraption on my groin.

"That looks painful," she says. "So are you serious? He went down at six-thirty? Before the twins went to sleep?"

It doesn't faze her at all. It is like I just showed her a new napkin holder.

"That's all you have to say?"

"I've come to expect this stuff."

Huh. This could be trouble. Have I lost the ability to shock Julie? The bar is getting pretty high if a restraining device for the genitals doesn't rattle her.

Julie does warm to the concept. Later that night, she dangles the key out the window, then pretends to drop it.

"Oops! Guess we'll have to call the locksmith."

Lying in bed, I tell her "I can't sleep. It's pinching."

"I'll let you free now—but only if you promise to put it on tomorrow."

"So you like the CB-3000?"

"I like the power. So sue me."

And I have to admit, the power suits her well.

CODA

This is Julie here. As part of being the obedient husband, A.J. asked if I would like to write the ending to get my point of view out there. Um, hell yeah! It's about time I got to get in my two cents.

This has been A.J.'s best experiment in, well, ever. I would like to take this moment to thank the readers who came up with it (although I'm still angling for "The Year of Giving My Wife Foot Massages" as a follow-up). For the sake of America's women, I hope this experiment starts a movement and other couples try it. Although if it does, I imagine A.J. will be hanged in effigy by the married men of America. Sorry, sweetie.

It really was one of the best months of our marriage, although I'm still annoyed that A.J. maneuvered to pick February to do this (and a nonleap year to boot!). Had he picked March, I could have gotten three more days of idol worship.

A.J.'s plan was that I'd eventually get bored of being in total charge and I'd be begging for his old self to come back. Guess what? That didn't happen. Maybe it would happen someday, but it would take a long, long, long time. I mean, husbands were in charge for thousands of years, right? I could last that long. Do I need him to agree with me on every little opinion about, for instance, movies or food? No. I like a spirited discussion. But do I enjoy having a yes-man when it comes to plans, wardrobe, and the household? Oh yes.

I do think that A.J. now appreciates me more. When I made the list of all the things I do, it was a revelation for him. For years, he seemed able to overlook the fact that if I weren't around, no bills would get paid, no sinks would get unclogged, no Pirate's Booty would get stocked.

I honestly believe he thought he was doing almost as much of the household management—that it was like 55/45 when in reality it was 80/20. I told him, it's going to be hard to get back to his old 80/20 ways now that the imbalance is so clear.

The experiment officially ended a couple of weeks ago when I made him find all the missing pieces to the kids' board games, which was a massive operation involving bookshelf-moving and rug-lifting. But even after deadline, he's continued to be a diligent househusband. Yesterday he filled the liquid soap dispensers. A big gold star.

I'm assuming there is some backsliding to come. I'm hoping for a final ratio of 60/40. A girl can dream, no?

I do believe that the experiment was good for our marriage. It made A.J.—and me—realize that it's not always about the big gesture. Marriage is an accumulation of the little gestures. The little gestures are the ones that count.

A.J. is right in that we got into a bad pattern of being sarcastic with each other. During this experiment, he was forced to say nice things. So then I said nice things. It was a vicious cycle of niceness!

I think we've kept some of that for now. I'd like to think that we've cut our sass by 35 percent on a good day. A.J. is always babbling on about how behavior shapes thoughts. It's his big mantra. In this case, I think it worked.

And, while I have your attention, I would like to point out that A.J. mysteriously left out some stuff. For starters, he was doing this ideal-husband experiment just when he had to turn the book in to the publisher.

And sometimes he'd try to weasel out of chores by saying, "I'm sorry but I'm on a big deadline." Um, excuse me, wasn't that the point, buddy? You can't prioritize anything over our marriage. That's the whole friggin' experiment!

At one point, he wanted me to come with him to a group marital therapy session for four hours on a Saturday. I reminded him that we had three children and we'd have to get a babysitter and Jasper would not be happy. He then suggested he go alone. He thought that would be a funny scene for the essay. Just him and all these couples. Uh, no.

He also asked if we could do a week where I follow everything *he* says—for contrast purposes. To which I replied, "I didn't sign up for that."

By the way, this is awesome. I am loving writing my point of view. I think I should suggest this for every experiment. It's the least he can do for turning me into a character. I live my life with everything on the record. Sometimes I'll say something, and I can see his eyes light up, and I'll think, Okay, that's going in the book.

In the past, he has given me censorship privileges but never annotations or rebuttals. With his first book, *The Know-It-All*, I nixed a couple of personal passages. Suffice it to say they were about my cycle. You're welcome, America.

But in this book and *The Year of Living Biblically*, I didn't change or delete anything (well, I did suggest changing the name of a friend in order to avoid a total confrontation—and, since A.J. hates confrontations, he was more than happy to oblige). It's so weird because I think I've gotten used to having my pri-

vate life out there. Besides, the e-mails that A.J. gets from readers reminding him that I'm a saint make it all worth it.

And despite the headaches, I do love him. The man, after all,
makes a decent chicken piccata.

POSTSCRIPT

Julie

Thank you very much. Though I am still aspiring that we reverse
roles for a week, so that I can command you for an experiment,
as discussed.

Love, AJ

P.S. This is Sunayana on behalf of A. J. Jacobs

$$Fame \leq Ego(x)^3$$

$$Zen + Focus = Productivity^2$$

$$\sqrt{Brain} \cdot Caveman = \frac{1}{x}$$

$$\frac{Outsourcing^8 + marriage}{12,000 \ miles} = q$$

$$x = \frac{Nudity + Public}{Dignity}$$

$$\sqrt{\frac{Nudity + Public}{Dignity}}$$

$$(Geo. \ Wash. - wig) \ Me = x$$

$$\int_b^a \frac{husband}{(wife) power}$$

$$\frac{Dating + Beauty}{x(Cyrano)} \neq Love$$

$$(wife) power^3 = x$$

$$\frac{Reason - Emotion}{Behavior} = Insanity$$

$$Truth^n - filter = Chaos$$

Chapter Ten

Do I Love My Wife?

How do I love thee? I love thee with serotonin produced by my raphe nuclei. I love thee with testosterone receptors deep in my hypothalamus. I love thee with dopamine that floods my primitive lizard brain.

Actually, I hope I love my wife with all my major brain parts—but who knows? The truth is, I don't know how I love her. That's the whole point of today's experiment. We'll see.

Right now, I'm stuck inside a whirring, clunking MRI machine at New York University. Six inches above my nose hovers an image of my smiling wife wearing a black spaghetti-strap dress.

In the adjoining room, two respected scientists are clicking computer keys and watching streams of data flow out of my skull and into their terminals. I stare at Julie's smile. I think about the most romantic moments in our courtship: kissing in the rain on West Seventy-seventh Street in Manhattan. The first time I reached over to hold Julie's hand—it was during a twee Irish film called *Waking Ned Divine*—and the joy I felt when she squeezed it back. The gondola ride in Venice. (*Really? Gondola? says one part of my brain. So clichéd. No, responds another, stay on task.*) "Okay, the romance phase is done," says one of the scientists. "Are you ready for sex?"

I think I love my wife. At least most of the time. (Not counting when she makes me go see Henry Jaglom movies.) But what does that mean—*I love my wife*? And how does my love stack up against other husbands'? For the first time in the history of human mating, scientists may have found a way to pin down this most ethereal of emotions. We're on the verge of dissecting this butterfly.

A handful of researchers, armed with MRIs, have begun to sift out the chemical mix that makes up love. "Until recently, we regarded love as supernatural," says Helen Fisher, a professor of anthropology at Rutgers who is one of the world's leading researchers on brain chemistry and sexual relationships and half of the team of scientists poking through my cranium. "We were willing to study the brain chemistry of fear and depression and anger but not love."

It's a controversial notion, that love can be reduced to a chemical cocktail. It gives conniptions to the Foucault types who see love as socially constructed.

Just think of the implications: If love is simply chemicals, doesn't that change its meaning? And how soon before we create a scientifically valid love potion? (Already under study, by the way.) What about a love vaccine to help us from falling for the wrong person? And if you have to rely on chemical enhancements, do you get an asterisk next to your name in the book of love, like Barry Bonds?

I've volunteered to be a guinea pig for two of the field's pioneers. In the past five years, Fisher and her research partner, neuroscientist Lucy Brown of Albert Einstein College of Medicine in New York, have put forty-nine crazy-in-love people into MRI machines to study their brains. I'm number fifty. But I'm the first *not* to be in the crazy-in-love, head-over-heels phase. I'm the first average married Joe they've ever studied.

When I told friends and family I was trying to scientifically assess my love for Julie, they all had the same response: "No good can come of this."

But knowledge is good, right? And if I understand how I love my wife, maybe I can learn how to love her better. I asked Julie if she would mind if I opened up my brain. She had the same reaction as when I suggested we go to Dave & Buster's restaurant and video arcade for our anniversary. "Fine," she sighed.

Inside the MRI tunnel, the image of my wife vanishes from the screen. And up pops another female face. This woman has the tip of her pinkie perched alluringly on her lips. Huge lips.

It's Angelina Jolie. That's another part of the experiment. The scientists and I want to see how my love for my wife compares with my feelings for Angelina Jolie.

I start to think of naughty things I want to do to Angelina Jolie. My eyes drift down to her cleavage. My neurons spit out dopamine. The machine whirs. *Hmm.* No good can come of this.

THE MACHINE

A quick word about this $2 million gadget that's trying to read my mind. The MRI is to brain science what Galileo's telescope was to astronomy. At least if you believe its proponents. Skeptics—and there are quite a few—question its accuracy as a guide to brain function, especially when dealing with individuals, as opposed to populations. They say that overenthusiastic researchers tend to read too much into the results, committing the scientific equivalent of seeing Jesus in a tortilla.

The fMRI (short for functional magnetic resonance imaging) captures 3-D movies of your brain to chart where the blood is flowing. When you speak, blood flows to the language centers. When you blink your eyes, it flows to the eye-blinking centers.

After studying the results over the years, Fisher has come up with a theory that love is created by three distinct brain systems—those for sex, romance, and attachment. She has described her findings in several books, most recently *Why Him? Why Her?* Here, an oversimplified version:

The Sex Drive. One of the main lust factories in the brain is a peach pit–size lump called the hypothalamus (deep in your skull, sitting just above the brain stem). This controls hunger and thirst. It also has receptor sites for testosterone, which fuels the sex drive in both men and women. So when you're feeling horny, the hypothalamus is working overtime. You don't have to be Richard Dawkins to figure out why evolution gave us the sex drive: Its job is to spread our DNA as widely and often as possible.

The Romance System. This produces the cocaine rush you get from beginning love. And cocaine is more than an idle metaphor. The reptilian brain—one of the nervous system's most ancient parts—floods you with dopamine, just as it does after you snort a line of blow. The dopamine gives you the same high, lack of sleep, delusional optimism, and obsessive thoughts. The great poet Robert Palmer was right: You can be addicted to love. Romance evolved so that you could focus your mating energies on appropriate partners—the most fertile woman, the best providing man.

The Attachment System. This is friendship on hyperdrive. While romance is thrilling, attachment is calming. It's created by a couple of hormones: vasopressin and oxytocin (not to be confused with Rush Limbaugh's painkiller OxyContin). Attachment evolved so that we could "tolerate our partners long enough to raise a kid together," says Fisher.

The three systems are intertwined. For instance, sex boosts attachment. When you have an orgasm, your brain pumps out oxytocin, heightening feelings of closeness. Which is why one-night stands often last past one night. And why exhausted married couples should force themselves to hump once in a while. In fact, semen itself contains oxytocin. You literally have a love syringe between your legs.

But the systems can often be distinct, Fisher believes. I will be the first human to test all three at once.

INSIDE THE MACHINE

It's a few days before the experiment, and I'm busy scouring photo albums in search of three perfect photos of my wife—one to spark each of the love systems. For the sex photo, I find a picture of my wife on the beach on our honeymoon. She's got her back to me and is looking over her shoulder. (Yes, that's her. The one with the partially exposed boob. Thank you for letting me print that, Julie.)

Later, Fisher tells me this is an echo of the classic "lordosis" pose favored by female animals. When female horses (or monkeys or pandas, etc.) want to mate, they raise their hips and look back over their shoulder at the male.

The attachment photo is harder. I choose one from a dinner for Julie's thirty-fifth birthday. Julie disapproves. "I have red eyes there. How can you find me attractive?"

"I think you look good."

"There are so many better ones."

"You're not allowed to argue," I tell her.

This is one of the huge side benefits of this project. Fisher told me that Julie and I can't get in a big fight before the test, lest it taint the results. This is, as Blagojevich says, a golden opportunity. Like this morning, Julie wanted me to take the early shift with our kids. I said it was her turn. She started to argue. "The MRI is coming up," I said, and rolled over.

In the end, Julie wins the attachment-photo argument. (That's her choice.)

On Thursday, I e-mail all three photos to Brown. And on Monday, I show up at NYU for my scan. I lie down on the table, and Fisher strokes my hand to calm me. She's very maternal. They slide me into the tunnel.

The images flash. I've got a list of scenarios to think about, depending on which photo is up. I've got romantic scenarios, attachment scenarios (picnic with the kids, watching *The Office* on the couch next to Julie), and sex scenarios. (I'll spare you.)

In between the images, Brown and Fisher try to clear the blood from my brain. The cleanser is a "neutral" face—a high school friend of Julie's who elicits overpowering boredom in me. (I can't show you.)

The entire exercise is at once scientific and voyeuristic. Like they're filming the most cerebral, least sexy porno in the history of the world.

Afterward, I fill out several questionnaires about my feelings toward Julie. *Do I get depressed when things don't go right with Julie?* Yes. *Do I think obsessively about Julie?* Not really.

THE RESULTS

A few days later, Brown e-mails me some initial findings. It's a great e-mail, full of exclamation points and capital letters. (*"OOOh, this is just too exciting . . ."*) It's also quite technical. I understand a good 40 percent of it. She e-mails again a few minutes later: *"I just read my message over again, and I'm not sure it's that coherent. Sorry. I'm excited."*

Later, I get a more polished report and do a debriefing with the scientists. It's interesting—the interpretation of the results isn't like reading a red or blue litmus paper. It requires art as well as science—skeptics would say more of the former. The major findings:

Romance: I'm not so addicted to love. The forty-nine human guinea pigs who went before me were all truly, madly, deeply in love. Some had just fallen in love. Some had just been dumped. (In a cruel twist of bioengineering, the romantic craving actually gets more intense postdumping.) And seventeen belonged to the small, freakish subset of people who claim they are still madly in love after years of marriage. These long-term romantics did, in fact, show cocainelike responses. I am not in that freakish subset. In fact, I'm one of the first of the fMRI guinea pigs *not* to show the rush from my lizard brain. This wasn't an honor I wanted.

Now, I'm not totally devoid of romance. Julie did fire up my prefrontal cortex, which is more intellectual, less visceral. "It's a more complex picture," says Brown. "Your brain is not just seeing pure reward, the way it is in the beginning of a relationship. Your brain is seeing some difficulties."

I tell Julie I don't have head-over-heels romantic feelings toward her.

"Shocker," she says.

"Why, you aren't head over heels in love with me?" I ask.

"Uh, no."

As part of the study, we'd each filled out questionnaires about how passionately we love each other. One of the questions was *Do you tremble when you see your lover?*

"So you don't tremble when you see me?" I ask her.

"No. Did you say you trembled?"

"A little. Sometimes."

"You so do not tremble."

She's right. I was just worried she'd see the questionnaire and get pissed.

Attachment: I love like a rodent of the grasslands. Scientists who study sex and love are totally smitten with prairie voles, a breed of overgrown mice that lives in dry parts of the Midwest. What's so special about prairie voles? They're basically monogamous—unlike the sluts and man-whores that make up 97 percent of mammals.

So if you want to study monogamy—and the government won't let you manipulate human love lives—you play God with the voles. Scientists do this by tweaking two brain chemicals—oxytocin and vasopressin. If you suppress the vasopressin system, normally faithful voles start acting like Eliot Spitzer. But if you boost the vasopressin in a promiscuous vole (such as the prairie vole's randy cousin the montane vole), it settles down with a mate. Vasopressin seems to be a key to attachment in male rodents. Oxytocin is the female equivalent. They do their job in a brain section called the ventral pallidum—which lit up when I was looking at a picture of Julie and one of my sons.

"There's lots of data on prairie voles about this area, but you're among the first humans to show this," says Brown. "It reveals this system may be conserved through mammals."

Like the voles, I have a strong attachment to my mate. It's hard to rank the three love systems, but it looks as if attachment is the winner for me, edging out sex and romance. And mine is a positive attachment, flavored with the dopamine pleasure drug. (You can be attached to someone and hate them.) This is reassuring information. On the other hand, I could block my vasopressin and be wenching in no time.

Sex: Against all odds, I'm still hot for my wife. Chemically, I'm at the most unmanly point in my life. A guy's testosterone drops when he gets married. (I'm nine years in.) It also drops when he has kids. (I've got three boys.) "Every time you cuddle with your children, you're likely to be driving down your testosterone," says Fisher. I can feel this. My sex drive is in neutral a lot of the time. Before the results came in, Brown told me to keep my expectations low. The sex regions might stay dark. She told me, "I actually think men in your situation"—meaning married with young kids—"should be encouraged to go to the Internet and look at pornography, because it brings novelty into the home. When you look at [porn], you're going to have some hormonal flooding. Which is needed in the 'captivity' situation."

And yet, according to the MRI, my libido is surprisingly strong. Looking at a sexy photo of my wife "activated part of your 'new brain' that represents the sensation of touch in your genital area," says Brown. "It's an interesting finding, because you said you had no erection." That's true. I had no erection. At my age, I need some soft music and small talk.

Even when I was in the romance phase of the test, the sex regions of the brain lit up. *This is beginning to look like quite a message for women,* Brown writes me. *Men always tell us that sex is important to them, that they are always thinking about it, it's always a factor when looking at women, but these data are making it really sink into my thick skull and take notice.*

You read it here first.

ANGELINA

Here's what my wife said when she found out she was going up against Angelina Jolie: "If you don't find Angelina more sexually attractive, there's something wrong with you." The results are in—and apparently there's something wrong with me.

Brown writes: *Julie and Angelina were exactly the same in areas associated with sexual arousal. Your midbrain thinks Julie is just as attractive as Angelina in the objective sense. But the romantic love isn't there for Angelina. Well, it's almost there for Angelina. Perilously close, in fact. But it doesn't make the cut.*

I do find my wife beautiful. But hotter than Angie? Like my wife, I'm not sure how to explain it. The measurements may be off. The researchers might be reading too much into the results. The MRI might have picked up the guilt and anxiety I felt when thinking about bradding Angie (and knowing my wife would see the results). Or . . . there's the lovely possibility that I *am* more sexually drawn to my wife.

THE CHINESE

A colleague of Fisher's did a study of newly-in-love Beijing couples. The results—though preliminary—are intriguing. The Chinese subjects were much more cautious about love than Americans. "They were more fearful about it, more careful about their emotions," says Brown. The research paper (written by Xiaomeng Xu and several collaborators) puts it this way: "The Chinese participants tended to associate love with negative features, e.g., heartbreak, and spontaneously listed more negative items than Americans, who associated love with more positive features, e.g., adoration."

The key brain region here might be the lateral orbital frontal cortex. This is a newer part of the brain, more intellectual, less instinctual, involved with weighing rewards and losses. And it fired up when both the Chinese and I thought about love.

This finding rings true. As I've gotten older, I've gotten more scared of love. I've come to see it as a dangerous emotion. I love the falling-in-love part. It's the falling-out-of-love part I can't stand. The paranoia, the depression, the aching, the gunfire.

Nowadays, if I had to sacrifice the highs to avoid the lows, I would. I'd prefer a mild emotional climate in my brain. Like the Bay Area. Fisher says she agrees with me. A few years ago, she says, "I was rejected horribly. I lost twenty pounds. My clothes looked ridiculous on me. I only had three hours of sleep at night. This is not all in fun. There's a lot of talk about the positive aspects of love. We as a society downplay the danger, the anxiety, and the disappointment. We romanticize romance." She adds, "Evolution really overdid it with the feeling of falling out of love."

CODA

So, in the end, how do I love thee?

"You do love your wife," says Brown. "It's just in a more complicated way. The way most people love their long-term spouses."

I love her, but not with the junkie's high. "But don't give up on that," says Fisher. "I think those children are going to grow up and you're going to have the experience of being madly in love." In fact, she and Brown want to put me back in the scanner each year for several years. "We want to determine the natural history of love relationships and the corresponding changes in brain systems within individuals."

I could even try to rev up the romance quotient for next year. Unfortunately, the best way to kick-start romance is by following that tiresome marital advice about doing exciting, novel, slightly dangerous things with your spouse. "Take a subway and get off at a random stop and eat at some dump that's the first place you see," suggests Fisher. It'll get the dopamine and testosterone flowing. Not good news for housebound schmoes like me.

Then again, legal love potions may be on the market soon.

That'd be easier. One company is already selling bottles of what they call Liquid Trust. It's an odor-free spray laced with oxytocin, the chemical that jacks up trust and attachment. I got a bottle sent to me at *Esquire* a few weeks ago. "It might work," says Brown, as she spritzed some on her hair, just in case. "It needs to be tested in a double-blind test." (In fact, that holds true for the whole field of reading brain fMRIs. It's a fascinating topic, but it's all very new, and should be approached with healthy skepticism in those frontal lobes.)

It's a weird feeling, trying to reduce love to organic compounds. Fisher's been doing it for years and is often asked if it takes all the fun out of love. She says no. "I can know every single ingredient in a piece of chocolate cake, but when I sit down to eat it, I can still feel the joy."

For me, translating love into biology is actually kind of reassuring. Yes, it takes away some of the mystery—but also the fear. Think of it like a drug: If you're high and feel like you're sliding off the face of the earth, you can tell yourself, *Hey, I'm having a horrible chemical reaction, but I'll get over it. I will stabilize.*

Plus, the MRI gave me some supposedly objective proof of my feelings. This comes in handy. Julie snaps at me today for forgetting to buy her oranges on the way home. She accuses me of being inconsiderate.

"Sorry," I say, "but it's a scientific fact that I love you."

And I've got 3-D images to prove it.

Author's Note

All the events in this book are true. Some of the sequences have been rearranged, and, in certain cases, the names and identifying details have been changed. Naturally, whenever possible, I tried to be radically honest.

Appendix A:
George Washington's 110 Rules
of Civility and Decent Behaviour in
Company and Conversation

PUNCTUATION AND SPELLING HAVE BEEN MODERNIZED.

1. Every action done in company ought to be with some sign of respect to those that are present.
2. When in company, put not your hands to any part of the body not usually discovered.
3. Show nothing to your friend that may affright him.
4. In the presence of others, sing not to yourself with a humming voice, or drum with your fingers or feet.
5. If you cough, sneeze, sigh, or yawn, do it not loud but privately, and speak not in your yawning, but put your handkerchief or hand before your face and turn aside.
6. Sleep not when others speak, sit not when others stand, speak not when you should hold your peace, walk not on when others stop.
7. Put not off your clothes in the presence of others, nor go out of your chamber half dressed.
8. At play and at fire, it's good manners to give place to the last comer, and affect not to speak louder than ordinary.
9. Spit not into the fire, nor stoop low before it; neither put your hands into the flames to warm them, nor set your feet upon the fire, especially if there be meat before it.
10. When you sit down, keep your feet firm and even, without putting one on the other or crossing them.
11. Shift not yourself in the sight of others, nor gnaw your nails.

12. Shake not the head, feet, or legs; roll not the eyes; lift not one eyebrow higher than the other, wry not the mouth, and bedew no man's face with your spittle by approaching too near him when you speak.

13. Kill no vermin, or fleas, lice, ticks, etc., in the sight of others; if you see any filth or thick spittle put your foot dexterously upon it; if it be upon the clothes of your companions, put it off privately, and if it be upon your own clothes, return thanks to him who puts it off.

14. Turn not your back to others, especially in speaking; jog not the table or desk on which another reads or writes; lean not upon anyone.

15. Keep your nails clean and short, also your hands and teeth clean, yet without showing any great concern for them.

16. Do not puff up the cheeks, loll not out the tongue with the hands or beard, thrust out the lips or bite them, or keep the lips too open or too close.

17. Be no flatterer, neither play with any that delight not to be played withal.

18. Read no letter, books, or papers in company, but when there is a necessity for the doing of it, you must ask leave; come not near the books or writings of another so as to read them unless desired, or give your opinion of them unasked. Also look not nigh when another is writing a letter.

19. Let your countenance be pleasant but in serious matters somewhat grave.

20. The gestures of the body must be suited to the discourse you are upon.

21. Reproach none for the infirmities of nature, nor delight to put them that have in mind thereof.

22. Show not yourself glad at the misfortune of another though he were your enemy.

23. When you see a crime punished, you may be inwardly pleased; but always show pity to the suffering offender.

24. Do not laugh too loud or too much at any public spectacle.

25. Superfluous compliments and all affectation of ceremonies are to be avoided, yet where due they are not to be neglected.

26. In putting off your hat to persons of distinction, as noblemen, justices, churchmen, etc., make a reverence, bowing more or less according to the custom of the better bred, and quality of the persons. Among your equals expect not always that they should

begin with you first, but to pull off the hat when there is no need is affectation. In the manner of saluting and resaluting in words, keep to the most usual custom.

27. 'Tis ill manners to bid one more eminent than yourself be covered, as well as not to do it to whom it is due. Likewise he that makes too much haste to put on his hat does not well, yet he ought to put it on at the first, or at most the second time of being asked. Now what is herein spoken, of qualification in behavior in saluting, ought also to be observed in taking of place and sitting down, for ceremonies without bounds are troublesome.

28. If any one come to speak to you while you are sitting, stand up, though he be your inferior, and when you present seats, let it be to everyone according to his degree.

29. When you meet with one of greater quality than yourself, stop and retire, especially if it be at a door or any straight place, to give way for him to pass.

30. In walking, the highest place in most countries seems to be on the right hand; therefore, place yourself on the left of him whom you desire to honor. But if three walk together the middest place is the most honorable; the wall is usually given to the most worthy if two walk together.

31. If anyone far surpasses others, either in age, estate, or merit, yet would give place to a meaner than himself in his own lodging or elsewhere, the one ought not to except it. So he on the other part should not use much earnestness nor offer it above once or twice.

32. To one that is your equal, or not much inferior, you are to give the chief place in your lodging, and he to whom it is offered ought at the first to refuse it, but at the second to accept though not without acknowledging his own unworthiness.

33. They that are in dignity or in office have in all places precedency, but whilst they are young, they ought to respect those that are their equals in birth or other qualities, though they have no public charge.

34. It is good manners to prefer them to whom we speak before ourselves, especially if they be above us, with whom in no sort we ought to begin.

35. Let your discourse with men of business be short and comprehensive.

36. Artificers and persons of low degree ought not to use many ceremonies to lords or others of high degree, but respect and highly

honor them, and those of high degree ought to treat them with affability and courtesy, without arrogance.

37. In speaking to men of quality do not lean nor look them full in the face, nor approach too near them at least. Keep a full pace from them.

38. In visiting the sick, do not presently play the physician if you be not knowing therein.

39. In writing or speaking, give to every person his due title according to his degree and the custom of the place.

40. Strive not with your superior in argument, but always submit your judgment to others with modesty.

41. Undertake not to teach your equal in the art himself professes; it savors of arrogance.

42. Let your ceremonies in courtesy be proper to the dignity of his place with whom you converse, for it is absurd to act the same with a clown and a prince.

43. Do not express joy before one sick in pain, for that contrary passion will aggravate his misery.

44. When a man does all he can, though it succeed not well, blame not him that did it.

45. Being to advise or reprehend any one, consider whether it ought to be in public or in private, and presently or at some other time; in what terms to do it; and in reproving show no signs of choler but do it with all sweetness and mildness.

46. Take all admonitions thankfully in what time or place soever given, but afterwards not being culpable take a time and place convenient to let him know it that gave them.

47. Mock not nor jest at any thing of importance. Break no jests that are sharp, biting, and if you deliver any thing witty and pleasant, abstain from laughing thereat yourself.

48. Wherein you reprove another be unblameable yourself, for example is more prevalent than precepts.

49. Use no reproachful language against any one; neither curse nor revile.

50. Be not hasty to believe flying reports to the disparagement of any.

51. Wear not your clothes foul, or ripped, or dusty, but see they be brushed once every day at least and take heed that you approach not to any uncleanness.

52. In your apparel be modest and endeavor to accommodate nature, rather than to procure admiration; keep to the fashion of your

equals, such as are civil and orderly with respect to time and places.

53. Run not in the streets, neither go too slowly, nor with mouth open; go not shaking of arms, nor upon the toes, kick not the earth with your feet, go not upon the toes, nor in a dancing fashion.

54. Play not the peacock, looking every where about you, to see if you be well decked, if your shoes fit well, if your stockings sit neatly and clothes handsomely.

55. Eat not in the streets, nor in the house, out of season.

56. Associate yourself with men of good quality if you esteem your own reputation; for 'tis better to be alone than in bad company.

57. In walking up and down in a house, only with one in company if he be greater than yourself, at the first give him the right hand and stop not till he does and be not the first that turns, and when you do turn let it be with your face towards him; if he be a man of great quality walk not with him cheek by jowl but somewhat behind him, but yet in such a manner that he may easily speak to you.

58. Let your conversation be without malice or envy, for 'tis a sign of a tractable and commendable nature, and in all causes of passion permit reason to govern.

59. Never express anything unbecoming, nor act against the rules moral before your inferiors.

60. Be not immodest in urging your friends to discover a secret.

61. Utter not base and frivolous things among grave and learned men, nor very difficult questions or subjects among the ignorant, or things hard to be believed; stuff not your discourse with sentences among your betters nor equals.

62. Speak not of doleful things in a time of mirth or at the table; speak not of melancholy things as death and wounds, and if others mention them, change if you can the discourse. Tell not your dreams, but to your intimate friend.

63. A man ought not to value himself of his achievements or rare qualities of wit; much less of his riches, virtue or kindred.

64. Break not a jest where none take pleasure in mirth; laugh not aloud, nor at all without occasion; deride no man's misfortune though there seem to be some cause.

65. Speak not injurious words neither in jest nor earnest; scoff at none although they give occasion.

66. Be not froward but friendly and courteous, the first to salute, hear and answer; and be not pensive when it's a time to converse.

67. Detract not from others, neither be excessive in commanding.

68. Go not thither, where you know not whether you shall be welcome or not; give not advice without being asked, and when desired do it briefly.

69. If two contend together take not the part of either unconstrained, and be not obstinate in your own opinion. In things indifferent be of the major side.

70. Reprehend not the imperfections of others, for that belongs to parents, masters, and superiors.

71. Gaze not on the marks or blemishes of others and ask not how they came. What you may speak in secret to your friend, deliver not before others.

72. Speak not in an unknown tongue in company but in your own language and that as those of quality do and not as the vulgar. Sublime matters treat seriously.

73. Think before you speak, pronounce not imperfectly, nor bring out your words too hastily, but orderly and distinctly.

74. When another speaks, be attentive yourself and disturb not the audience. If any hesitate in his words, help him not nor prompt him without desired. Interrupt him not, nor answer him till his speech be ended.

75. In the midst of discourse ask not of what one treats, but if you perceive any stop because of your coming, you may well entreat him gently to proceed. If a person of quality comes in while you're conversing, it's handsome to repeat what was said before.

76. While you are talking, point not with your finger at him of whom you discourse, nor approach too near him to whom you talk, especially to his face.

77. Treat with men at fit times about business and whisper not in the company of others.

78. Make no comparisons and if any of the company be commended for any brave act of virtue, commend not another for the same.

79. Be not apt to relate news if you know not the truth thereof. In discoursing of things you have heard, name not your author. Always a secret discover not.

80. Be not tedious in discourse or in reading unless you find the company pleased therewith.

81. Be not curious to know the affairs of others, neither approach those that speak in private.

82. Undertake not what you cannot perform but be careful to keep your promise.

83. When you deliver a matter do it without passion and with discretion, however mean the person be you do it to.

84. When your superiors talk to anybody hearken not, neither speak nor laugh.

85. In company of those of higher quality than yourself, speak not 'til you are asked a question, then stand upright, put off your hat, and answer in few words.

86. In disputes, be not so desirous to overcome as not to give liberty to each one to deliver his opinion and submit to the judgment of the major part, especially if they are judges of the dispute.

87. Let your carriage be such as becomes a man grave, settled, and attentive to that which is spoken. Contradict not at every turn what others say.

88. Be not tedious in discourse, make not many digressions, nor repeat often the same manner of discourse.

89. Speak not evil of the absent, for it is unjust.

90. Being set at meat scratch not, neither spit, cough, or blow your nose except there's a necessity for it.

91. Make no show of taking great delight in your victuals. Feed not with greediness. Eat your bread with a knife. Lean not on the table, neither find fault with what you eat.

92. Take no salt or cut bread with your knife greasy.

93. Entertaining anyone at table it is decent to present him with meat. Undertake not to help others undesired by the master.

94. If you soak bread in the sauce, let it be no more than what you put in your mouth at a time, and blow not your broth at table but stay 'til it cools of itself.

95. Put not your meat to your mouth with your knife in your hand; neither spit forth the stones of any fruit pie upon a dish nor cast anything under the table.

96. It's unbecoming to stoop much to one's meat. Keep your fingers clean and when foul wipe them on a corner of your table napkin.

97. Put not another bite into your mouth 'til the former be swallowed. Let not your morsels be too big for the jowls.

98. Drink not nor talk with your mouth full; neither gaze about you while you are drinking.

99. Drink not too leisurely nor yet too hastily. Before and after drinking wipe your lips. Breathe not then or ever with too great a noise, for it is uncivil.

100. Cleanse not your teeth with the tablecloth, napkin, fork, or knife, but if others do it, let it be done with a pick tooth.

101. Rinse not your mouth in the presence of others.

102. It is out of use to call upon the company often to eat. Nor need you drink to others every time you drink.

103. In company of your betters be not longer in eating than they are. Lay not your arm but only your hand upon the table.

104. It belongs to the chiefest in company to unfold his napkin and fall to meat first. But he ought then to begin in time and to dispatch with dexterity that the slowest may have time allowed him.

105. Be not angry at table whatever happens and if you have reason to be so, show it not but on a cheerful countenance especially if there be strangers, for good humor makes one dish of meat a feast.

106. Set not yourself at the upper of the table but if it be your due, or that the master of the house will have it so. Contend not, lest you should trouble the company.

107. If others talk at table be attentive, but talk not with meat in your mouth.

108. When you speak of God or His attributes, let it be seriously and with reverence. Honor and obey your natural parents although they be poor.

109. Let your recreations be manful not sinful.

110. Labor to keep alive in your breast that little spark of celestial fire called conscience.

Appendix B:
List of Cognitive Biases

A few words about this list. First, it's not meant to be a comprehensive list—the brain has dozens of other quirks I didn't include. This is just a Whitman's Sampler of the biases I found to be most interesting and/or influential. I assembled the list from such books as *Nudge, Predictably Irrational, Sway,* and *The Science of Fear.* And also Wikipedia, which, objectively speaking, has impressive coverage of cognitive biases. In fact, a lot of the descriptions, phrasings, and examples are taken directly from Wikipedia (though I checked them with alternate sources to make sure they were correct). In a few cases, I came up with the name for the bias myself. This happened when an author or researcher described the phenomenon but didn't label it, or else labeled it with a highly technical name. (These entries are marked with an asterisk.)

And finally, so as not to cause undue bias against biases, I should mention that these biases aren't necessarily bad. Often they are. Often they lead us to form harmful stereotypes or make terrible decisions. But in many situations, these biases can be useful. Like the Bandwagon Effect. Following the crowd may not always be right, but it is often the most efficient way to make a decision.

Anchoring—When we're estimating the value of something, we give too much weight to the first number we hear.

Availability Fallacy—Our lazy mind gloms on to the most vivid, emotional examples. When we think of danger, we think of hideous plane crashes or acts of terrorism. Even though boring old cars kill eighty-four times more people.

Bandwagon Effect—We are overly influenced to behave and think like the majority. It's why the Billboard Hot 100 list is self-perpetuating.

Bias Blind Spot—We fail to compensate for those biases that we're aware of. (In other words, even behavioral economists fall for biases.)

The Big Man Bias—A person with authority is perceived to be taller than he or she is. In one study, subjects estimated a man was 2.5 inches taller when he was introduced as a professor instead of as a student.*

Choice-Supportive Bias—The tendency to retroactively ascribe positive attributes to an option one has selected. In other words, we are master rationalizers.

Conjunction Fallacy—Take this test from Amos Tversky and Daniel Kahneman, two giants in the field.

Linda is thirty-one years old, single, outspoken, and very bright. She majored in philosophy. As a student, she was deeply concerned with issues of discrimination and social justice and also participated in antinuclear demonstrations. Which is more probable?

A: Linda is a bank teller.

B: Linda is a bank teller and is active in the feminist movement.

If you're like 85 percent of people, you chose option B. Even though it couldn't possibly be more probable, because it's more specific than A. That's the conjunction fallacy.

Consistency Bias—Remembering your past opinions and behavior as resembling present opinions and behavior—even though they don't.

Contrast Effect—We overestimate something if it happens right after we experience a contrasting stimulus. If you lift a fifty-pound sack of bricks, then lift a ten-pound sack of bricks, the ten-pound sack will feel feather-light.

The Creaking Bridge Effect—Our tendency to confuse general excitement and/or fear with sexual excitement. I got the name from an experiment involving an attractive woman asking men to take a poll. If the poll was given on a dangerously creaky footbridge, the men were much more likely to hit on the woman than if the poll was given on steady ground.*

The Decoy Effect—When you prefer Option A over Option B thanks to the introduction of Option C. The key is that Option C is a lesser version of Option A. As Dan Ariely says, if you go out to a bar, try bringing along two friends: One who is good-looking but looks nothing like you, and one who is an uglier version of you. You'll get a lot more attention.

Distinction Bias—When we see two options side by side, we overestimate their differences. For example, when TVs are displayed next to each other on the sales floor, the difference in quality between two very similar, high-quality TVs may appear huge. So you might shell out a lot more for the higher-quality TV, even though the difference in quality is imperceptible when the TVs are viewed in isolation.

Endowment Effect—If we own something, we think it's more valuable than if we don't own it.

Extremeness Aversion—Our tendency to avoid extremes, being more likely to choose an option if it is the intermediate choice. It's why we never order the least or most expensive wine. (As Homer Simpson says, "Waiter, a bottle of your second-least expensive champagne.")

Forer Effect—The reason why we so often fall for horoscopes and carnival mind-readers. It's our tendency to think that vague, general descriptions that would fit any personality are accurate descriptions of our personality. *Yes, I do sometimes get angry but then often forgive people later. How did you know?*

Framing Effect—We make different choices about the same situation depending on how it's presented. You might undergo surgery with a "95 percent survival rate," but avoid surgery with a "5 percent mortality rate."

Fundamental Attribution Error—When explaining another person's behavior, we give too much weight to his or her personality and too little to the situation. If a flight attendant is rude, we're quick to say she's "a bitch," without taking into account situational factors (e.g. maybe her mom is dying, maybe her husband cheated on her, etc.).

Gambler's Fallacy—The belief that the past can influence a random event. In other words, if you toss a coin, and it comes up heads ten times in a row, and you say "Next time, it's got to be tails," you've just committed the Gambler's Fallacy.

Halo Effect—If we like one aspect of a person, the positive feeling spills over into other areas. It's why we think good-looking people are virtuous and smart.

Hindsight Bias—The belief that something was more predictable than it was. In more colloquial terms, "hindsight is 20/20." How could we have missed the signs that Pearl Harbor was coming? Because there was lots of conflicting intelligence.

Ikea Effect—We overvalue an object if it was difficult to assemble. Buy a friend a table that requires assembly and he'll like it more.

Illusion of Control—Our tendency, as Wikipedia puts it, "to believe we can control or at least influence outcomes that we clearly cannot." In other words, most of my life.

Illusory Correlation—When you falsely believe that two things are linked. For example, many of us believe that we always choose the slow line at the grocery. But that's only because we remember the slow lines, not the fast ones.

Just World Phenomenon—Our tendency to believe that the world is "fair" and people get what they deserve. Frankly, to me, this is the most depressing bias. I desperately want to believe that people get what they deserve. But Ecclesiastes is right: The race does not go to the swift. Bad things happen to good people.

Lake Wobegon Effect—Our brains are delusively cocky. We all think we're better-looking, smarter, and more virtuous than we are. (It's named for Garrison Keillor's town, where "all the children are above average.")

Law of Similarity—If X and Y look similar, humans believe they are somehow related, whether they are or not.

Mere Exposure Effect—Our tendency "to express undue liking for things merely because we are familiar with them," as Wikipedia says. It's why I brushed with Crest for twenty years.

Name Narcissism—The preference for words that begin with the same letter with which your name begins. (Maybe my surname is why I married Julie and named my son Jasper.)*

Not-Invented-Here Syndrome—The tendency to discount products and solutions that were created by other people.

Omission Bias—The tendency to judge harmful actions as worse, or less moral, than equally harmful inactions.

Out-Group Homogeneity Bias—"Our tendency to see members of our own group as being relatively more varied than members of other groups," in the words of Wikipedia. It's the bias behind statements like "they all look the same to me."

Overconfidence Effect—You are correct far less often than you think you are (related to the Lake Wobegon Effect). It's especially true for hard tasks. In spelling tests, subjects were correct about 80 percent of the time when they were "100 percent certain."

The Palmolive Effect—We irrationally link physical cleanliness to moral cleanliness. For instance, handwashing lessens our sense of guilt. A study showed that subjects who washed while feeling guilty were less likely to compensate for their guilt later by donating to charity.*

Patternicity—The tendency to find meaningful patterns in meaningless noise (seeing the Virgin Mary in a tortilla, for instance).

Planning Fallacy—Our tendency to underestimate task-completion times. Or why I thought that I would finish this book in December when I finished it in May. Actually, June.

Primacy Effect—The tendency to weight initial events more than subsequent events. Why first impressions are unduly powerful.

The Pygmalian Effect—A type of self-fulfilling prophecy: A student will perform better if the teacher expects him or her to do so. The opposite is called the Golem Effect, where low expectations lead to bad performance.

Reactance—The cognitive bias that dominates our teen years. We sometimes have the urge to do the opposite of what we've been told to do simply because we want to resist a perceived incursion on our freedom of choice.

Recency Effect—The tendency to weight recent events more than earlier events. (Psychologist Daniel Gilbert talks about this with regard to his memory of *Schindler's List*. He remembers not liking the whole movie. Even though he did like most of it, he just didn't like the ending—a fact he didn't realize until he rewatched the movie.)

Reminiscence Bump—Your memory overrepresents events that happened when you were ten to twenty-five years old, deemphasizing events that happened in other periods of life.

Romeo Bias—Men generally overestimate a woman's sexual interest in them. (As Ariely points out, this is a good evolutionary strategy. It's better to err on the side of delusional than miss opportunities.)*

Rosy Retrospection—We often rate past events more positively in retrospect than we rated them when they occurred. This especially occurs with moderately pleasant effects, like vacations, when the minor annoyances fade from memory. In other words, "the good old days" are a myth.

The Scrooge Effect—The tendency to be more generous when you're full and more stingy when you're hungry. It's why fund-raisers should always ask for money after the rubber-chicken lunch.*

Self-serving Bias—When you attribute your successes to internal factors but attribute your failures to situational factors beyond your control. As in, *I got an A because I worked hard.* Whereas, *I got an F because the teacher doesn't like me.*

Serial Position Effect—It's easier to remember items near the end of a list and the beginning of the list. Those poor items in the middle are often forgotten.

Source Amnesia—We forget where we learned a fact. Facts learned in *The Wall Street Journal* gain as much credulity as a "fact" learned from your cousin's barber.

Spontaneous Trait Transference—Why you should avoid trash-talking. "People will unintentionally associate what I say about the qualities of other people with my own qualities. So if I told Jean that Pat is arrogant, unconsciously Jean would associate that quality with me." (From Gretchen Rubin's book, *The Happiness Project*.)

Sunk Cost—We allow costs that can't be recovered to irrationally influence our decision. If you buy a movie ticket, then find out from Rotten Tomatoes that it's almost surely going to be terrible, but you still go to the theater and suffer through it in order to avoid "wasting" money, you've fallen for sunk-cost thinking

Supply Closet Effect—We find it easier to justify stealing if we're not stealing cash. It's more palatable for us to steal pens and envelopes from the supply closet than it is to steal the equivalent in dollars. The farther removed something is from cash, the easier it is for us to steal.*

Swag Bias—Our tendency to take free stuff, whether or not we want it. It's why my apartment is still cluttered with promotional computer mouse pads from conventions, even though I don't use a computer mouse.*

Telescoping Effect—The fancy name for how memories move to the middle distance. We move recent events backward in time and remote events forward in time, so that recent events appear to be more remote, and remote events, more recent.

Unit Bias—The irrational urge to finish an entire unit, such as a plateful of food.

Valence Effect—The tendency to overestimate the chance that good things will happen.

Von Restorff Effect—An item that "stands out like a sore thumb" is more likely to be remembered than other items. For instance, if a person examines a shopping list with one item highlighted in bright green, he or she will be more likely to remember the highlighted item than any of the others.

Zeigarnik Effect—People remember uncompleted or interrupted tasks better than completed ones. Russian psychologist Bluma Zeigarnik first studied the phenomenon after noticing that waiters seemed to remember orders only as long as the order was in the process of being served. (Some life hacker sites suggest taking advantage of this quirk when studying for a test. Take frequent breaks in which you play games or go for a walk, so you remember the unfinished material better.)

Zero-Risk Bias—When we crave the complete elimination of Risk A, even if that creates an increase in Risk B. Wikipedia cites the "Delaney clause of the Food and Drug Act of 1958, which stipulated a total ban on synthetic carcinogenic food additives. The 'total ban' was a zero-risk policy that actually led to health risks due to exposure to older, probably more dangerous food additives that continued to be used."

Notes

Dedication

vii *Courtney Holt:* Who is Courtney Holt? He's a guy I met at a dinner party. The night I met him, he was talking about how much he loved Wii Fit. At the time, the only way to buy the much-in-demand game was to line up outside a certain midtown store at 6 A.M. so you could get one of the dozen or so units released that day. I casually mentioned that if he scored me a Wii Fit, I'd dedicate my next book to him. Two days later I got a huge box in the mail. And . . . well, Courtney: I'm fulfilling my side of the bargain. Thank you for my Wii Fit.

Introduction

xiii *have transformed my life:* Regarding the issue of transformation, I'm sometimes asked if my Bible experiment or encyclopedia experiment had any long-lasting effects. The answer is yes to both, but more so with the Bible project.

That year changed me more deeply than anything since going through puberty (an experience that also involved odd facial hair growth, come to think of it). It changed me in ways large and small. Perhaps most notably, it's given me a sense of gratitude. Thanksgiving is a huge theme in the Bible, and I got carried away saying prayers of gratefulness. (I'd be thankful the elevator came when I pressed the button, thankful it didn't plunge to the basement when I stepped inside, and on and on.) I've tried to retain that point of view. I try (emphasis on the word *try*) to be thankful for the one hundred little things that go right every day instead of focusing on the three or four that go wrong—which has been a radical shift in perspective. Every night, I spend several minutes listing some of the things for which I'm grateful. I ask Jasper to do this as well—though he's always thankful for the same three things: Wii bowling, Wii baseball, and Wii golf. It's a start, anyway.

I also try to keep the Sabbath. I'm a convert to the idea that we need a sanctuary in time (something I talk about in the Unitasker essay as well). I don't observe Shabbat in the Orthodox Jewish sense—I still flick on and off lights on Saturdays—but I try my hardest not to check e-mail or talk on the phone.

In my daily life, I still sin all the time. But . . . I think I sin about 30 or 40 percent less than I used to. One of my big battles is with gossip. My biblical year taught me that gossip, though it's mighty tasty, as the Bible says, can be shockingly corrosive. If you cut down on negative speech, it changes the way you think. You begin to have a more optimistic view of the human species. Which I really need these days.

I'm still agnostic, but after my year, I did end up joining a synagogue in our neighborhood. It's reform. And we don't go very often. But Julie and I did join. And for now, Julie and I are sending our kids to the synagogue's day school. I actually don't care if my sons grow up to be hard-core atheists or steadfast observers, as long as they are good people. Menschen, if you will. But I thought it'd be nice to give them a little taste of religion so that they can make a decision for themselves.

The result is, Jasper now knows more Hebrew than I do. It's kind of disorienting. He'll come home and I don't know whether he's spouting the usual four-year-old nonsense words, or if he's saying a blessing.

As for the encyclopedia book, one of the most long-lasting effects was to fuel my curiosity. It gave me a little appetizer-sized taste of all these fascinating topics, and inspired me to try to keep on ingesting knowledge.

I can't say I remember everything I read in the encyclopedia. I've forgotten, oh, 99 percent of it. But in my defense, 1 percent of the encyclopedia—that's still a whole bunch of information. I still have way too many facts rattling around in my brain. I know this because no matter what I see, it somehow triggers a fact. It's like a sickness. I'll see a cat, and I'll think of how the Egyptians made mummies of their cats—but they also made mummies of mice so that the cats would have something to eat in the afterlife. Very considerate. Oh, and no matter how hard I try, I still can't forget that René Descartes had a fetish for cross-eyed women.

Chapter 1: The Unitasker

5 *Multitasking costs the economy $650 billion a year, according to the Institute of Pulling Numbers Out of Its Ass:* Actually it's from Jonathan B. Spira, chief analyst at a business research firm called Basex, as quoted in Walter Kirn's *Atlantic* article.

28 *Nietzche's writing changed:* The observation about how Nietzsche's writing style changed after he started using a typewriter is from "Is Google Making Us Stupid" in the *Atlantic*. Thanks to Google for that one.

30 *"Daddy! Daddy!" "Can't talk now," I responded:* In *The Year of Living Biblically*, I mentioned that when he was two years old, Jasper was behind the curve, vocabulary-wise. For the record—and in case Jasper ever reads my books—I want to say that he's now fully caught up and speaks like a young William F. Buckley Jr.

Chapter 2: My Outsourced Life

36 *Sexiest Woman Alive:* For those who are wondering. Jessica Biel was named *Esquire*'s sexiest woman that year. And yes, she does like swordfish!

36 *I outsource a whole mess of online errands to Asha:* Asha also signed me up for Netflix, and I outsourced my movie picks to her. She did pretty well. Her first five choices were:

Man on Fire (not usually my kind of movie, but really sharp)
Catch Me If You Can (a great tale)
Minority Report (If I hadn't seen it in the theater, it'd be a good choice.)
The Terminal (I didn't love it, but I'm glad I saw it.)
Patch Adams (I didn't love it, and I'm not glad I saw it.)

45 *an entry in Wikipedia:* Sadly, Honey's edits to my Wikipedia entry were removed by stern Wikipedians who called them "nonsense" and "generally unencyclopedic."

47 *My team is good:* Another reason I loved my outsourcers is that they could be forceful when called for. Theirs was an extremely polite and diplomatic variety of force, but still, very impressive. I remember wondering if an article I'd edited might be mentioned on the magazine's cover. So Honey wrote to the art director: "If we add two lines of text about this sizzling scene, it would make the layout attractive. It

might also serve as an 'eye-catcher.' I'm sure you would like this idea. However, the entire decision does vest upon you."

And finally, if you're interested in outsourcing your own life, here are some options:

- GetFriday.com: This is the division of Your Man in India that was founded after the article came out. To sign up, you can e-mail support@getfriday.com. Prices vary, but in one plan you pay ten dollars a month for the service, plus fifteen dollars an hour for the tasks.
- Brickwork: the company that employed Honey. You can reach them at info@brickwork.com. Their website is www.b2kcorp.com/.
- If you want to work with a U.S.-based company, you can try Do My Stuff (www.DoMyStuff.com). This is sort of like a cross between Craigslist and eBay. You post a task, and assistants put in a bid to work on it. I've never used it myself, so I can't vouch for its quality, but it's an interesting idea.

Chapter 3: I Think You're Fat

57 *Ass Crack, Virginia:* That's a lie. I actually said "Butt Fuck, Virginia," but the chapter was so obscenity-filled already, I censored myself on the page.

69 *do* not *want to have a playdate:* The fuller story—which I recounted in *The Year of Living Biblically*—is this:

Julie, Jasper, and I went to a local hot dog joint and sat next to another family.

"Julie Schoenberg?" asked the ponytailed mom.

It was an acquaintance Julie hadn't seen since college. Hugs were exchanged, compliments toward babies extended, spouses introduced, mutual friends discussed.

At the end of the meal, we got our check, and Julie's friend said, "We should all get together and have a playdate sometime."

"Absolutely," said Julie.

"Uh, I don't know," I said.

Julie's friend laughed nervously, not sure what to make of that.

Julie glared at me.

"You guys seem nice," I said. "But I don't really want new friends right now. So I think I'll take a pass."

Brad Blanton talks about the scary thrill of total candor, the adrenaline rush. I felt that. I heard myself saying the words, but they seemed unreal, like I was in an off-Broadway production.

Julie was too angry to look in my direction.

"It's just that I don't have enough time to see our old friends, so I don't want to overcommit," I said, shrugging. Hoping to take the edge off, I added: "Just being honest."

"Well, I'd love to see you," said Julie. "A.J. can stay home."

Julie's friend pushed her stroller out of the restaurant, shooting a glance over her shoulder as she left.

CHAPTER 4: 240 MINUTES OF FAME

73 *"You're a clue":* I couldn't figure out a way to search *New York Times* crossword puzzles, so "forty-eight down" is a guess. If anyone knows the real number, please let me know.

76 *send me to the Oscars:* I wasn't the only *Entertainment Weekly* writer at the Oscars that year. When I worked there, *EW* got a handful of tickets for the reporters. One ticket went to me, another to Jessica Shaw, who acted as my publicist during the night. Jessica did double duty, actually getting quotes from nonfake celebrities.

79 *Julia's vanity production company:* To be fair, Julia Roberts's production company, called Shoelace Productions, did have partial involvement in producing a couple of movies, most notably *Stepmom.*

81 *Would the actresses be willing:* I'm still grateful and amazed my bosses at *Entertainment Weekly* allowed me to propose via the *Sex and the City.* It's one reason I can be glad I didn't work at *The New Yorker.* Would Seymour Hersh be allowed to ask Rahm Emanuel to make a video for his son's bar mitzvah?

82 *The headphones are tuned:* My inadvertent eavesdropping on Kim Cattrall had a fictional parallel in the romantic comedy *Notting Hill.* Hugh Grant's character visits Julia Roberts's character on the set of her new movie, and hears her trash-talking him over his wireless headphones. Their story ended more happily than mine and Kim's.

87 *An opposing study argues:* The alternate thesis—that narcissists flock to show business in the first place—can be found in the book *The Mirror Effect: How Celebrity Narcissism Is Seducing America,* by Dr. Drew Pinsky and S. Mark Young. The authors came to their conclusion after questionnaires filled out by celebrities revealed they were huge narcissists even at the start of their careers. Reality stars were the most narcissistic, by the way. Musicians, the least.

CHAPTER 5: THE RATIONALITY PROJECT

90 *But then I read a book:* The coauthor of *Nudge,* Cass Sunstein, is my first cousin, once removed. Which probably makes me irrationally biased toward him.

91 *In the kitchen, I find Julie:* Julie may be irrational sometimes, as we all are. But she can also be the most rational person I know. She had no qualms about taking a flight just three weeks after 9/11. I wouldn't go within a mile of an airport. But in retrospect, she was more rational. *The Black Swan* has an interesting section on all the deaths caused by the increase in car traffic after 9/11.

97 *an astounding number of superstitions:* If you want to understand superstitions better, I'd recommend looking to B. F. Skinner's pigeon trick. Skinner was the Harvard psychologist famous for two things: attempting to reduce almost all human behavior to stimulus and response, and raising his daughter in a laboratory box (the second is an urban legend).

I'm no Skinnerian behaviorist when it comes to humans, but I think his pigeon trick provides a helpful analogy to understanding superstitions, and the confirmation bias in general. I learned about it from *Believing in Magic: The Psychology of Superstition,* by Connecticut College professor Stuart A. Vyse.

Okay, here's the trick:

Before a speech, Skinner would put a pigeon in a cage. The cage was rigged so that at regular intervals, without fail, a food pellet would drop down a chute into the cage. Nothing the pigeon did could make the food come slower or faster. It was all based on clockwork. So Skinner would bring the cage into a lecture, then put a cloth over it and put the cage to the side. An hour later, he'd finish his speech and unveil the pigeon.

Invariably, the pigeon would be exhibiting some zany behavior. It'd be walking in circles. Or pecking furiously at the floor. Or bobbing its head like a white guy at a jazz club. See, the pigeon had come up with a cockamamie theory that its head bobbing had caused the food to drop. So it continued doing it, fueled by the confirmation fallacy.

My version of nutty pigeon behavior comes in many varieties: swallowing in pairs or repeatedly touching the faucet, for instance. Pretty much everyone I know engages in magical thinking, in this illusion of control. It's just a matter of to what degree.

I called Vyse to talk to him about it. The exchange I remember best was this:

"I notice you say in the book that superstitious people are associated with lower intelligence."

"It's a very slight correlation," he said.

"But it's there?"

"Yes. But it's very slight."

To make me feel better, Vyse told me that at Harvard, there's a statue of patron John Harvard, and there's a superstition that you'll get a good grade if you touch his left foot before an exam. "The foot is entirely worn off."

CHAPTER 7: WHAT WOULD GEORGE WASHINGTON DO?

130 *strange obsession with his compost pile:* The John Adams manure fact is a reference to something I learned while reading the encyclopedia. As I said in *The Know-It-All:* ". . . the strangest passage ever published in *Britannica*'s history is about John Adams, in the section on his retirement. It says he spent his time writing letters, 'enjoying his tankard of hard cider each morning before breakfast' and 'rejoicing at the size of his manure pile.' Now, it's moderately strange that the second president of the United States was sloshed before breakfast. But that he derived joy from the size of a pile of excrement? I just don't know how to interpret that. It occurs to me, though, that this might make for a nice monument to this American hero—a marble replica of his twenty-foot-high manure collection. Take that, Mount Rushmore!"

139 *I'm doing my best to walk around New York like George Washington:* I should mention that, unlike my biblical year, when I wandered the Upper West Side in a robe and sandals, I didn't spend a lot of time sporting a tricornered hat. I only did it once, for the photo that appears at the start of this chapter. I expected that going out in public in my Colonial costume to be an afternoon of jeers, mockery, and agape mouths. But it was actually quite pleasant. The most memorable feedback I got was to be saluted by two different strangers. New Yorkers respect our Founding Fathers. (The outfit—rented from Creative Costume Company in midtown New York—was also really comfortable, perhaps because of the elastic waistband, which may not have been totally authentic.)

Incidentally, attire wasn't a minor thing to Washington. He wasn't exactly a dandy, despite the fact that he owned yellow gloves. Dandyism would violate Rule 54: "Play not the peacock, looking every where about you, to see if you be well decked . . ."

But it's fair to say he was preoccupied with external appearances. He knew the clothes can make the man. Washington designed his own outfits, as Burns and Dunn point out, right on down to the "width of lapels and placement of all 12 buttons."

And he was the only one who showed up to the Second Continental Congress decked out in his military uniform. Which meant that when it came time to appoint the commander of the military, well, Washington was already dressed for the occasion. As Jack Donaghy on *30 Rock* says: "Dress for the job you want, not the job you have."

CHAPTER 8: MY LIFE AS A BEAUTIFUL WOMAN

160 *How about Internet dating:* In case it helps any online daters, I present the extended list of my instant deal breakers:

Pirate talk in the opening e-mail (One guy wrote "Avast ye matey! I'm comin' aboard.")
User names that contain allusions to the Kennedy assassination (e.g., Zapruder, unless the guy happens to be named Zapruder)
The suitor demanding a fast reply, because he only has one day left on his free trial (I got that several times.)
The suitor using the same opening line he used a month ago, oblivious to the fact that he'd failed the first time. Namely: "Your pic brightened my day. The rest of the day was terrible—I lost my cell phone on the Long Island Rail Road. LOL!" He apparently loses his cell phone a lot.

CHAPTER 9: WHIPPED

193 *just about twice a week, according to several recent surveys:* It's actually a complicated question—the one about how often married couples have sex. It differs according to age, health, and country. More information can be found here: http://family.jrank.org/pages/1102/Marital-Sex-Sexual-Frequency.html.

Bibliography

CHAPTER 1: THE UNITASKER

Bernstein, Jeffrey. *10 Days to a Less Distracted Child*. New York: Marlowe, 2007.

Bodian, Stephan. *Meditation for Dummies*. Hoboken, N.J.: Wiley, 2006.

Conley, Dalton. *Elsewhere, U.S.A.* New York: Pantheon, 2009.

Crenshaw, Dave. *The Myth of Multitasking*. San Francisco: Jossey-Bass, 2008.

Davich, Victor. *8 Minute Meditation*. New York: Perigee, 2004.

Hallowell, Edward M., and John J. Ratey. *Driven to Distraction*. New York: Touchstone, 1994.

Jackson, Maggie. *Distracted: The Erosion of Attention and the Coming Dark Age*. Amherst, N.Y.: Prometheus, 2008.

Lieberman, Matthew D., et al. "Putting Feelings into Words: Affect Labeling Disrupts Amygdala Activity in Response to Affective Stimuli," *Psychological Science*, June 2007.

Medina, John. *Brain Rules*. Seattle: Pear, 2008.

Nadeau, Kathleen, and Ellen B. Dixon. *Learning to Slow Down and Pay Attention*. Washington, D.C.: Magination, 2004.

Posner, Michael, and Mary Rothbart. *Educating the Human Brain*. New York: APA, 2006.

Wallace, B. Alan. *The Attention Revolution*. Somerville, Mass.: Wisdom, 2006.

CHAPTER 3: I THINK YOU'RE FAT

Blanton, Brad. *Beyond Good and Evil*. Stanley, Va.: Sparrowhawk, 2006.

——. *Honest to God*. Stanley, Va.: Sparrowhawk, 2001.

——. *Practicing Radical Honesty*. Stanley, Va.: Sparrowhawk, 2000.

——. *Radical Honesty*. Stanley, Va.: Sparrowhawk, 2005.

——. *The Truthtellers*. Stanley, Va.: Sparrowhawk, 2004.

Frankfurt, Harry G. *On Bullshit*. Princeton, N.J.: Princeton University Press, 2005.

CHAPTER 4: 240 MINUTES OF FAME

Braudy, Leo. *The Frenzy of Renown*. New York: Oxford University Press, 1986.

Elkin, Stanley. "In Darkest Hollywood." *Harper's*, December 1989.

Halpern, Jake. *Fame Junkies*. Boston: Mariner, 2008.

Pinsky, Dr. Drew, and S. Mark Young. *The Mirror Effect*. New York: Harper, 2009.

CHAPTER 5: THE RATIONALITY PROJECT

Aamodt, Sarah, and Sam Wang. *Welcome to Your Brain*. New York: Bloomsbury USA, 2008.

Ariely, Dan. *Predictably Irrational*. New York: Harper, 2008.

Brafman, Ori, and Rom Brafman. *Sway: The Irresistible Pull of Irrational Behavior*. New York: Doubleday, 2008.

Fine, Cordelia. *A Mind of Its Own*. New York: Norton, 2008.

Gardner, Daniel. *The Science of Fear*. New York: Dutton, 2008.

Gilbert, Daniel. *Stumbling on Happiness*. New York: Knopf, 2006.

Kida, Thomas E. *Don't Believe Everything You Think*. Amherst, N.Y.: Prometheus, 2006.

Howard, Martin. *We Know What You Want*. New York: Disinformation Company, 2005.

Lehrer, Jonah. *How We Decide*. New York: Houghton Mifflin, 2009.

Marcus, Gary. *Kluge: The Haphazard Construction of the Human Mind*. New York: Houghton Mifflin, 2008.

Packard, Vance. *The Hidden Persuaders*. Brooklyn, N.Y.: Ig, 2007.

Pink, Daniel H. *A Whole New Mind*. New York: Riverhead, 2006.

Rushkoff, Douglas. *Coercion: Why We Listen to What "They" Say*. New York: Riverhead, 1999.

Taleb, Nassim Nicholas. *The Black Swan: The Impact of the Highly Improbable*. New York: Random House, 2007.

Thaler, Richard H., and Cass R. Sunstein. *Nudge: Improving Decisions About Health, Wealth, and Happiness*. New York: Penguin, 2008.

Vyse, Stuart. *Believing in Magic.* New York: Oxford University Press, 1997.

Walker, Rob. *Buying In.* New York: Random House, 2008.

Zimbardo, Philip. *The Lucifer Effect.* New York: Random House, 2008.

CHAPTER 7: WHAT WOULD GEORGE WASHINGTON DO?

Brookhiser, Richard. *What Would the Founders Do?* New York: Basic Books, 2006.

Burns, James MacGregor, and Dunn, Susan. *George Washington.* New York: Times Books, 2004.

Caldwell, Mark. *A Short History of Rudeness.* New York: Picador, 1999.

Day, Nancy. *Your Travel Guide to Colonial America.* Minneapolis: Runestone, 2001.

Ellis, Joseph J. *His Excellency: George Washington.* New York: Knopf, 2004.

Fleming, Thomas. *Washington's Secret War.* New York: HarperCollins, 2005.

Hawke, David Freeman. *Everyday Life in Early America.* New York: Harper & Row, 1988.

Hemphill, C. Dallett. *Bowing to Necessities.* New York: Oxford University Press, 1999.

Johnson, Paul. *George Washington: The Founding Father.* New York: Harper Perennial, 2009.

Rees, James, with Stephen Spignesi. *George Washington's Leadership Lessons.* Hoboken, N.J.: Wiley, 2007.

Smith, Richard Norton. *Patriarch: George Washington and the New American Nation.* New York: Houghton Mifflin, 1993.

Unger, Harlow Giles. *The Unexpected George Washington.* Hoboken, N.J.: Wiley, 2006.

Washington, George. *Rules of Civility.* Ed. Richard Brookhiser. Charlottesville: University of Virginia Press, 2003.

CHAPTER 9: WHIPPED

Belkin, Lisa. "When Mom and Dad Share It All." *New York Times,* June 15, 2008.

Coontz, Stephanie. *Marriage, a History.* New York: Penguin, 2006.

Dowd, Maureen. *Are Men Necessary?* New York: Putnam Adult, 2005.

Faber, Adele, and Elaine Mazlish. *How to Talk So Kids Will Listen &* *Listen So Kids Will Talk*. New York: Avon, 1999.

Fisher, Helen. *Why We Love*. New York: Henry Holt, 2004.

Glover, Robert A. *No More Mr. Nice Guy!* Philadelphia: Running Press, 2003.

Gray, John. *Men Are from Mars, Women Are from Venus*. New York: HarperCollins, 1992.

Hochschild, Arlie Russell, with Anne Machung. *The Second Shift*. New York: Penguin, 1993.

Schwartz, Pepper. *Love Between Equals*. New York: Free Press, 1994.

Acknowledgments

There's an irrational brain quirk called the "Egocentric Bias," which causes an individual to overestimate his or her contribution to a joint project and underestimate others' contributions.

No way I'm falling for that. Which is why I'm about to go on an epic thanking spree. So here goes:

Thank you to Marysue Rucci, my editor at Simon & Schuster, who is brilliant, funny, inspiring, and also patient with deadlines.

Thanks to Sloan Harris at ICM, a great agent whose civility rivals George Washington's.

Thanks to David Granger, the visionary editor of *Esquire*, in whose magazine some of these essays had their start. And to Peter Griffin, who edited some of these essays for *Esquire* and made them a hell of a lot better.

Thanks to Rob Weisbach, without whom I wouldn't be a writer.

There are an absurd number of people to thank at Simon & Schuster: the unflappable Julia Prosser, Nicole De Jackmo, Victoria Meyer, Aileen Boyle, Lisa Healy, Marcella Berger, Jackie Seow, Amy Cormier, Leah Wasielewski, and Sophie Epstein, one of the greatest e-mailers I know. Thanks to my bosses, David Rosenthal and Carolyn Reidy, for the unwavering support.

I'm indebted to all who read the manuscript and gave me their wisdom, namely: Shannon Barr, Neely Harris, Andrew Lund, Kevin Roose, David Katz, Brian Raftery, John Podhoretz, Lily Percy, Jeffrey Engel, Candice Braun, Lynette Vanderwarker, Gary Rudoren, Gretchen Rubin, Paul Mandell, Roger Bennett, Peter Martin, Chad Millman, and Albert Kim.

I'm grateful to those who helped focus my thoughts about focusing—Maggie Jackson and John Fossella.

Thanks to the patriotic staff at Mount Vernon, especially James Rees, Mary Thompson, and Melissa Wood.

Thanks to Nigel Parry and F. Scott Schafer for the images.

Thanks to APB's Ken Eisenstein, Jonathan Braverman, and Linda Braverman. And to the rational minds of Cass Sunstein, Richard Thaler, and Dan Ariely.

Thanks to many others at ICM, including Josie Freedman and Kristyn Keene.

Thanks again to my understanding family—my mom, dad, sister, father-in-law, step in-laws, nieces, nephews, and all three brothers-in-law—for allowing me to turn their private lives public.

Thanks to my mother-in-law, who made the right decision about her apartment.

Thanks, above all, to my preternaturally saintly wife, Julie, and our three wonderful guinea pigs, Jasper, Zane, and Lucas.

About the Author

A. J. Jacobs is the author of two *New York Times* bestsellers: *The Know-It-All* and *The Year of Living Biblically*. He is the editor at large at *Esquire* magazine. A.J. has written for the *New York Times*, *Washington Post*, and *Entertainment Weekly*, and is an occasional correspondent for National Public Radio. He lives in New York City with his wife, Julie, and their children. You can visit his website at www.ajjacobs.com.

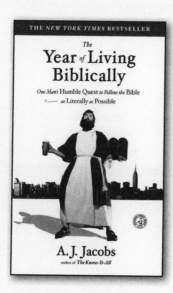